"Eric Worre's *Go Pro* has become the de facto bible of network marketing. Eric takes his more than 25 years experience in the profession and boils it down to nuts and bolts practical wisdom you can learn and apply. If you want to succeed, if you are serious about being a network marketing professional, make this book the centerpiece of your library!"

Chris Widener, Author of The Art of Influence

"Simple and surgical reading for new or experienced entrepreneurs. A book that helps to grow the quality of behaviors and results in our community commerce industry. *Go Pro* is a must!"

Bruno Grilo, Million Dollar a Year Earner, Monavie

"I have read so many books written on our amazing profession, but *Go Pro* is one of the very best. Eric validates the power of network marketing plus gives practical scripts and language to help build your business. This book cuts straight to the point and is easy to understand. Whether you are part-time or full-time in our profession, it is a must-read. Thank you Eric for creating a simple tool to help everyone succeed."

Kathy Coover, Owner of Isagenix International

"Eric hit it square on the head with *Go Pro*. Honestly, the title says it all. If you want to become a professional in network marketing, then his book is a must-read. That means non-negotiable. If I want to become a pro, it is a requirement to read *Go Pro*. Get his book now! This book is already destined to become an all-time classic for our profession."

Todd Falcone, Network Marketing
Speaker, Coach, and Trainer

"*Go Pro* should be required reading for every new network marketer. The strategies and scripts Eric Worre details in this book are as solid and proven as they get. Regardless of which company you're with, this book will give you the key to achieving financial and lifestyle freedom in network marketing."

Matt Morris, Million Dollar a Year earner and
Best-selling Author of The Unemployed Millionaire

"The chapter titles alone represent a blueprint for success in network marketing. Eric is a master teacher. He focuses on core fundamentals that work and he keeps it simple. His story about the 'game plan interview' can single-handedly propel your residual income to the next level. This is a must-read for anyone who wants to go pro in this business."

Kody Bateman, Founder and CEO of
SendOutCards and Author of MLM Blueprint®

"Congratulations to Eric Worre and *Go Pro*! Eric is a modern-day Jim Rohn, with the best communication skills to help people see there is a better way. Eric is the only one I recommend to my entire organization around the world, to attend or purchase everything that he offers. The seven steps in *Go Pro* are the key to becoming a professional, and is a must-read for everyone on my team. We teach leaders to buy more books to help duplicate, teach and train their leaders to learn how to develop their skills, and to create more value in their own profession. Thanks, Eric, for reminding everyone network marketing is a profession. Keep up the good work you're doing on Network Marketing Pro—the profession needs your shows and my team thanks you for them!"

Jim Fobair, Network Marketing Legend,
Unicity Chairman's Club, Triple Diamond

"*Go Pro* by Eric Worre is the best vehicle for people to understand how to succeed in network marketing. We use it daily to change people's lives. After we put the book in our starter kit, our entire company has grown dramatically."

Frank Bjordal, Admiral Director and Eqology CEO

"There has not been a relevant, powerful book written on how to build a network marketing/direct-sales empire in 20 years, and Eric Worre's *Go Pro* was long overdue. No one is better qualified by a long shot to write this book. Eric has built several enormous empires himself, but more importantly, has interviewed dozens of top sales leaders in our profession—in-depth interviews digging for all the key distinctions that led to their elite success—all captured on video. *Go Pro* is the preeminent book on mastering our profession. Period."

Richard B. Brooke, Author **Mach II, The Art of Vision and Self-Motivation,** *and* **The Four Year Career,** *Founder, BlissBusiness.com*

"I first met Eric Worre at an industry event where he was the keynote speaker in 2004. I was instantly impressed by his experience and willingness to give a new guy like me the real goods. It was refreshing to listen to a trainer who actually had experience at the top of the game. I wondered why he didn't have a book back then. I left that event inspired by Eric and decided to follow his advice. In the following decade I've made millions in the business because of what I learned at that event. I was excited to get an advance copy of *Go Pro*. It is the sage advice I expected from Eric. Every story in this book is real. I've read the book several times now. If there was only one book that you could read as a road map to success in direct sales, *Go Pro* could easily be that book."

Ken Dunn, Million Dollar a Year Earner

"I have been in the Network Marketing profession as both a Distributor and also on the corporate side for many years now and I recommend Eric Worre's *Go Pro — 7 Steps to Becoming a Network Marketing Professional* to everyone that I work with, on either side of the table. This is simply one of the most powerful tools you can put into somebody's hands who wants to get results in their business. It has all of the information that anyone needs to really go pro. It is like having your very own master trainer in your pocket, as Eric reveals all he has learned and applied in his 20-plus years in this profession. I personally keep copies of this amazing resource on hand all the time and gift these to distributors around the world when I visit many countries. Whether you are brand new to this profession, or a veteran of many years, Eric's book will still hold something for you. *Go Pro* will become one of those stories we hear about in years to come of how this one simple book changed so many lives."

Casey-Lea Edwards, V.P. b:hip Global

"Eric's book is the best I've read on how to build a network marketing business, since joining the profession 23 years ago."

Todd Smith, $25 Million Dollar Earner

"Anyone looking to create a professional income in network marketing and direct sales deserves to read *Go Pro*. This profession can liberate people like no other, and with the skills that Eric delivers in his book, you cannot miss."

Susan Sly, Author, Speaker, and
Seven-Figure Income Earner

"Twenty years ago Eric Worre made a decision to become a Network Marketing Pro. At this moment of decision, everything changed. Eric has not only spent years studying the profession from the top people in our field, he has put what he learned into practice. Eric has interviewed and become friends with hundreds of the best network marketers in the world. His book is simple, concise and will prove to be one of the most practical network marketing guidebooks of all time. I love *Go Pro* and recommend it to everyone who wants to be a professional network marketer."

Jordan Adler, Network Marketing
Millionaire and Author of **Beach Money**®

"There is a skillset that needs to be mastered to achieve the success you desire, whether it's in direct selling, affiliate, or network marketing. Eric's book *Go Pro* shortens that learning curve dramatically and is really a must-read for anyone serious about success."

BK Boreyko, Vemma Owner & CEO

"In my opinion, *Go Pro* is the best book I've ever read on how to build a network marketing business. It's a no-nonsense collection of facts, not theories, that will help beginners understand the correct way to get started and build a big business. The book is also a great tool for professional networkers, as it's full of proven duplicable methods to ensure your organization continues to thrive. Eric Worre has done what no one else has been able to do — write a manual for building a network marketing business. If you want to get PRO results in network marketing, read the book and make sure your entire organization does as well!"

Mike Sims, Multi-Million Dollar Earner

"I have known Eric Worre for a number of years, and of course I knew of him as a peer in the profession for many years prior to our personal acquaintance. The depth of his knowledge and understanding of our industry and the requirements for participant success become immediately apparent to the reader of *Go Pro*. There are a handful of simple skills required to succeed in our profession. The knowledge that must be a precursor to the development of these skills can be gained by the student of *Go Pro*. When one over time combines the skills outlined in *Go Pro* with positive character attributes that cause others to seek association with us, we have progressed far towards getting the key in the lock to success in our great industry. Want to really succeed? *Go Pro*."

Randy Schroeder, Million Dollar Earner

"Finally! *Go Pro* is the book our industry has been waiting for! It not only validates the legitimacy and power of the network marketing profession, but it gives the newest person specific direction and training on how to become really good in this business! It took me many, many years to learn what you can learn in one reading of *Go Pro*!"

Tom Alkazin, Multi-Million Dollar Earner

"Eric has really empowered every network marketer with this powerful, easy to understand guide on several of the most important fundamentals of our business. Recruiting can really be this easy, once we understand how to do it right and practice at keep it this simple. Every networker should read this book at least once every three months."

Brian Carruthers, Million Dollar Earner

"Eric Worre's *Go Pro* lives up to its title — a captivating book taking the reader through the world of becoming a true professional in network marketing! Eric's real life experience comes to life, providing an abundance of insight and a practical step-by-step guide that will shave years off your learning curve. *Go Pro* is a fantastic resource to both aspiring networkers as well as seasoned professionals. A must-read!"

Joshua Denne, Multi-Million Dollar Earner

Go Pro

7 Steps to Becoming a Network Marketing Professional

Eric Worre

Network Marketing Pro™

ISBN 978-0-9886679-0-7

For information on quantity discounts or on having this title customized for your company, please email the publisher at gopro@networkmarketingpro.com.

Requests for permissions should be addressed to the author at Network Marketing Pro, Inc., 800 E. 1st Street, Suite 310, Wichita, KS 67202, 1-855-66GOPRO, or via email, gopro@networkmarketingpro.com.

Printed in the United States of America

*This book is dedicated
to the Network Marketing
Distributor. Thank you for
having the courage
to follow your dreams.*

Contents

About Network Marketing Pro

NetworkMarketingPro.com was created in 2009 to be a FREE resource to help educate and elevate the Network Marketing Profession. You can find hundreds of free training videos, million dollar earner interviews, and other valuable information at **http://networkmarketingpro.com.**

We also welcome you to join our community on Facebook:

http://facebook.com/nmpro

We would be honored if you could take a few moments and write a review of this book on Amazon.

For information on printing a custom edition of *Go Pro*, email gopro@networkmarketingpro.com.

BULK DISCOUNT PROGRAM: Our goal is to get this book into the hands of as many people as possible. To make this goal a reality, we have created a bulk discount program that will allow leaders to have quantities of *Go Pro* on hand at all times. We encourage you to:

- Get books into the hands of every person on your team
- Give a copy to every new person who joins your organization
- Make copies available for sale at all of your events

1-9	$12 each	100-499	$6 each
10-24	$10 each	500-999	$5 each
25-49	$8 each	1,000+	$4 each
50-99	$7 each		

To order, visit www.networkmarketingpro.com/gopro. If you have questions, contact us at 1-855-66GOPRO, or via email at gopro@networkmarketingpro.com.

Acknowledgments

I'm not a writer. Let me tell you that up front. The journey that has led to this book has been a very long and winding road. In fact, I've attempted to do this a half dozen times and even hired a few ghostwriters to help out. But in the end, it never felt just right, so I guess you're stuck with me offering it to you in my own words.

I'm not the best Networker either. There are people much better than I am, although I've had what most people would call a wildly successful career. I do believe I've developed a knack for figuring out what the super successful people do and delivering it in a way that can be easily understood.

Network Marketing has its own "jargon." Some companies call their people distributors, others are team members, and still others are brand partners, promoters or associates.

Whether it's the name of a distributor or any of the other jargon in our business, please don't let that distract you as you read this book. Focus on the concepts, not the names. Concepts never change, while names change all the time.

As we start this journey together, there are a few important people I need to thank.

To my wife Marina, God blessed the world the day you were born, and He blessed me the day I finally found you.

To my children, Taylor, Alexandra, Daniela, Chandler, and Domenic, and my grandson Ethan, I'm so proud of all of you. I have no doubt you will do great things in this world.

To my parents and the rest of my extended family, I can't thank you enough for all your love and support throughout my entire life. I love my family.

To the thousands of friends around the world, you've become my true extended family. I've heard it said that "friendship is wealth." I think that's true, and because of you, I'm a wealthy man.

To Chad Porter, Network Marketing Pro wouldn't function without you. Thank you for all the hard work and dedication. I appreciate you so much.

To Melody Marler Forshee, thank you for being my editor and helping to organize this book. I couldn't have done it without you.

And to the Network Marketing Profession, thank you for saving my life back in 1988. You made me become a better man, and I'll be forever grateful.

Introduction

I remember the day I was introduced to Network Marketing for the first time. It was January 1988. I was 23 years old and selling real estate for a small company owned by my father and his friend John Joyce.

I was newly married with a little boy. I was already behind on my bills, and I was scared. The year before I had earned about $45,000 in real estate commissions, which was a good thing. The problem was that I had spent about $60,000, and didn't save any money to pay my taxes, which would be due in just a few months.

When John Joyce came to my desk that day and said, "Eric, I think I have a way for us to make some extra money," I said, "Tell me more!" He went on to say a good friend of his had something to show us and had invited us to his house. So I got in the car with John and my dad and drove over to check it out.

When we arrived, he brought us into his living room, popped a tape into his VCR and hit PLAY. I sat and watched this crazy video. It was filled with mansions and limousines and testimonials of people making fortunes virtually overnight. It was so over the top I just couldn't believe it to be true so I proceeded to tell everyone I thought it was a bad idea and I wasn't interested. My natural mental filters just couldn't let it in.

Then something interesting happened. John and my dad said, "Okay, that's too bad. We're going to do it anyway."

This had a MAJOR impact on me because the only thing worse than being broke and in debt was the thought of seeing these two go on to make huge money without me! So, I changed my attitude, pulled my dad aside, and asked him if he would loan me some money to sign up. Thank God he said yes, because deciding to become a Network Marketing distributor completely changed my life.

When I got started, I treated my business like most people do, which is to say I didn't treat it like a business at all. I got in, made some phone calls, and hoped my timing and positioning was enough for me to get lucky and make a few bucks. And at first it worked! I DID make some money, and it was very exciting, although I have to disclose something to you. For those first few months, my entire strategy was to quickly call all of my dad's contacts before he had time to get to them. I thought if I called them, told them my dad and John Joyce were involved, and got them to a meeting or to watch a video, then if they were interested my dad wouldn't fight over who got credit, since I was in his organization. I had limited success with this, but as you can imagine, it didn't last long.

So three months after I got started, my Network Marketing income dried right up. And when it did, my positive attitude completely went away. I started to blame everything and everyone for my lack of success. My upline wasn't giving me enough help. The company didn't provide adequate training. I didn't know enough people. No one would respect me because I was so young. I blamed the product. I blamed the company. I blamed the economy. I blamed everyone but myself.

But I had a big problem. Blaming the world wasn't helping to pay my bills. And I had walked away from real estate after that first commission check. It was going to take too long to get a real estate commission and I had no college degree, so getting a decent paying job was out of the question. The only place I could go to create some cash flow was back to Network Marketing.

So I put my head down and went to work. At first it wasn't easy. In fact, in my first three years I rebuilt my organization seven times! I'd build it up and it would crash and I'd build it up again and it would crash. Over and over and over again.

After those three years, I was more than discouraged. I'd almost lost hope. Then something happened that changed my life. Actually it was a combination of two things. It was the night before a company convention and I was watching a news program on television. They had a guest who was an expert on a topic I can't recall now. What went through my mind was, "How does a person become an expert on THAT topic?" The only thing I could think of is they must have decided to become experienced, learn everything they could, read every book, talk to every other person, and learn it so completely that they became an expert.

The next day I went to the company convention and watched superstar after superstar walk across the stage. And then, it was like being hit by lightning. It finally clicked in my brain that if I truly decided to do it, I could become an expert at Network Marketing. I could focus on the skills. I could practice until I became an expert, and NO ONE could stop me.

Up until that moment, I was always looking for an angle. I was hoping to get lucky. I was hoping to sponsor that one superstar who was going to change everything. And I was scared I would lose my chance if it didn't happen soon.

In an instant, everything changed. I realized I didn't have to worry about getting lucky. Timing and positioning were nice, but not necessary for my long-term success. I didn't have to worry about my upline, knowing the right people, or anything else. All I had to do was become an expert.

So I decided that day to change my focus and develop the skills to become a Network Marketing Professional. It was a day that changed my life.

Since then, my life has been an amazing adventure. Network Marketing became a career for me. I have complete time freedom. I've met the most amazing people around the world. I've been able to touch and be touched by the lives of hundreds of thousands of people, travel all over the world, contribute to the causes that are important to me and most importantly, become a better person in the process.

All of this happened for me and it can happen for you too. In this book, I'm going to give you the fundamental principles that can guide you to becoming a Network Marketing Professional. They have served me well over the past few decades and I know they will serve you just as well.

Welcome to an exciting new adventure!

CHAPTER ONE

Network Marketing Isn't Perfect...It's Just BETTER.

Do you feel restless? Do you feel unsatisfied? Do you feel there must be a better way when it comes to your work and the way you make your living?

The good news: There IS a better way, but it's different than what you were taught in school. Let me explain.

As I travel and speak around the world, I like to play an audience participation game. I ask people to help me create the ultimate business and to tell me specific things they'd like to have in that business and things they'd like to avoid. It always makes for a very interesting list. If we were face to face, I'd do the same thing with you now. But since we're not, let me summarize what people from over 30 countries have told me while creating what I like to call "The Perfect Career List."

People usually start naming things they don't want:

- No boss
- No commute
- No alarm clock
- No employees
- No politics
- No compromises
- No discrimination
- No educational requirement

And then, as people start to use their imaginations in a more positive way, they start to visualize some positive attributes:

- Something positive
- Great product or service
- Unlimited income
- Residual income
- Enjoy the people you work with
- Time freedom
- Something meaningful

- Personal growth
- Lots of perks
- International
- Contribution to worthy causes
- Low risk
- Low start-up costs
- Economy-proof
- Tax benefits
- Fun!

Now, you might add some attributes of your own, but wouldn't you agree that's a pretty good start? Imagine being able to enjoy a career with all those attributes!

All "jobs" that I know of fall into one of five categories:

- Blue-collar
- White-collar
- Sales
- Traditional business ownership
- Investing

Blue-Collar Careers

Here is the Wikipedia definition of blue-collar. "A blue-collar worker is a member of the working class who performs manual labor." My definition is someone who labors to fix something, make something, clean something, build something, or service something (or someone).

In my life, I've worked many blue-collar jobs. And, for anyone who's ever engaged in this line of work, there is a certain satisfaction in a job well done.

But here's the big question: Can blue-collar work deliver on The Perfect Career List? The obvious answer is no. Sure, it can deliver on some of the attributes. It might have a great product and a low start-up cost or any number of other individual items on the list, but if you really look at it, blue-collar just can't get you where you want to be. Not "The Perfect Career."

White-Collar Careers

Here is the Wikipedia definition of white-collar.

"The term white-collar worker refers to a person who performs professional, managerial, or administrative work, in contrast with a blue-collar worker, whose job requires manual labor. Typically white-collar work is performed in an office or cubicle."

My definition is a person who is employed by someone else to do work other than manual labor or sales.

Many people choose a white-collar career, as it is one of the most socially acceptable of the options available. It has long been viewed as the safe and secure option. Recently that has changed. The implied contract that, if you are loyal to the company, the company will be loyal to you, is long gone.

I've also been a white-collar worker in my career. In my experience, there are two types of people who do this type of work: Achievers and Hiders.

Achievers are the people who want to perform at a high level. They are ambitious, motivated and energetic. They are full of ideas and want to move up the corporate ladder, which are great attributes to have. But there is a downside for the Achiever.

The moment a person decides to be an Achiever, they become a target. Their boss sees them as threatening to their job, so they start to hold them down or take shots at their reputation. Their peers see them as a person who will either embarrass them or keep them from getting a promotion, so they start to do what they can to undermine their accomplishments.

So, to remain an Achiever and survive in this hostile environment, a person must become good at one thing that has nothing to do with their productivity—and that's politics. They must learn how to navigate the political world by diminishing their enemies and strengthening their relationship with powerful people. In fact, some of the most successful people in the corporate world aren't Achievers at all. They are pure politicians.

So if you decide to work in the corporate environment and to be an Achiever, you must accept the fact that you must become a good politician also.

Now, let's talk about the Hiders. These are the people who HATE politics, but still need a job. They learn not to be the ambitious Achiever. They don't stand out. They don't speak up in meetings. They don't bring new ideas. They HIDE. They keep their heads down and do as they're told. They do just enough so that they aren't talked about negatively. They survive.

And this has worked for decades. But in the New Economy, it's becoming much more difficult to hide. And people are running out of time.

So, back to our Perfect Career List: Can a white-collar job deliver on the list? Again, the clear answer is no—certainly not in very many areas.

Sales

Some people choose to get away from being an "employee" and get involved in a sales career. This is certainly more adventurous because typically salespeople are paid on their production instead of by the hour.

I've known thousands of salespeople. There is a common theme I've noticed over the course of my career. The typical salesperson will have a period of time where everything goes perfectly. Everything they touch turns to gold and they make some really good money.

As soon as that happens, they almost always set their lifestyle to that level of income. They buy a new house, get new cars, put their kids in better schools, purchase a vacation home—the works. Everything is great for a while.

And then something changes.

The company changes the compensation plan, their territory gets reduced, a competitor shows up, they lose their best customer, the economy goes into recession, new technology makes their offer less valuable, or government regulations change their industry. These are just a few examples. There are hundreds more reasons why the salesperson's world could (and probably will) get more complicated.

When that happens, with the big lifestyle they've developed, now 40 hours a week isn't enough to pay the bills. So they go to 50 hours a week. And then 60. And then 70. And then their life gets very small. Yes, they have the stuff, but they don't have time to enjoy it.

The other challenge for the sales career is, no matter how a person does, they still start at zero the next day. It can be tiring to live under that kind of pressure over a long period of time.

Can a sales career pay the bills? Sure. But can it deliver on The Perfect Career we described earlier? Again, the answer is no.

Traditional Business Ownership

Some people opt for the big dream—building their own business where they are the boss and they call the shots. It's an exciting idea, isn't it? Here's the reality for most people:

Step one: They use their life savings, take on new debt, and many times borrow money from friends and family to get started.

Step two: They take on more debt in the form of leases and personal guarantees in just about every direction.

Step three: Now instead of focusing on what they are good at (let's say they were great at sales and decided to start their own business), they have to be all things to all people. They act as attorney for legal matters, accountant for financial matters, babysitter for employee matters, negotiator for purchasing matters, and collection agency for accounts receivable matters. They even get to take out the garbage. They are doing EVERYTHING but selling, which is what they were good at in the first place.

Step four: They struggle. Instead of owning the business, the business owns them. They are the first person to work and the last person to leave. And after everyone else gets paid, they might be able to take home enough money to pay their own bills, let alone reduce the debt they incurred to start the business in the first place.

Step five: They succeed or they fail. They either hit a point down the road where the business is successful, or they fail, many times filing for bankruptcy and falling back into a corporate or sales job. And even if they are successful, that usually means a lifetime of long hours and stress.

Sounds romantic doesn't it? If you haven't started your own business before, ask friends who have if this description isn't accurate. Most people who start their own traditional business aren't worried about getting a return on their investment. They just want a return OF their investment. It's pretty clear that traditional business ownership can't provide the Perfect Career as we've described it.

The Investor

The last category of ways to earn a living in the world today is to be an investor. And what do you need to become an investor? Money, right? If you don't have a lot of money, it's going to be very difficult to earn a living from the return on your investments, especially if you try to be conservative to reduce the risk of loss.

But let's say you do. What's the next thing you need in order to be a successful investor? You need to have incredible knowledge and skill. I know more people than I could count who were skillful real estate investors over the years. But when things radically changed in the real estate market, their skill couldn't help them. They lost big.

Would you like to invest in someone's traditional small business? Good luck. In most cases, you won't be an investor; you are more likely to be a philanthropist.

How about the stock market? People do great there, don't they? A few do, at least from time to time. But I know more people who've lost than have won, especially in the past decade. It's very difficult to have guaranteed returns when you're not in control. And trust me, as an investor you are NOT in control. Anything can happen. And it can happen overnight.

Let me tell you a story to illustrate that point. In late 2001, I was living large. I had sold a company I co-founded and was working as a very highly paid consultant. For my part of the sale I received approximately 170,000 shares of stock in the new company. It was publicly traded on the New York Stock Exchange and selling for about $44 a share, which meant the value of my stock was around $7.5 million. I had big income and a great portfolio. Life was GOOD.

I used part of the stock to secure a home construction loan of about $2 million for a dream house I was building. As for the rest, I didn't diversify because I knew the company was in great shape with a good product and an amazing sales force.

Then something out of my control happened. Overnight the stock went to $37 a share because a group of investors had targeted the company and shorted the stock. In other words, the lower the stock price went, the more money they would make.

I thought it was ridiculous because the company was doing great, so I bought some more shares at $37, using my existing shares as collateral, knowing the price would go back up. It went to $33. I bought more shares. It went to $27. I started getting margin calls, which meant if I didn't send them money, they were going to start selling my shares to cover the losses. I didn't have it to send.

The stock continued to go down. It went all the way to $10 a share and my $7.5 million was gone. Poof! All in less than 90 days. Now, the stock eventually came back and the company was taken private for $65 a share. But I wasn't there to capitalize on it. I was wiped out.

Could I have been smarter? Sure. Did I make mistakes? Absolutely. But here's the lesson: If you're going to be an investor, you have to accept that things will be taken out of your control from time to time. And when that happens, it can be very expensive.

So, back to our Perfect Career List. Can being an investor deliver on that list? I don't think so.

We've talked about blue-collar work, white-collar work, sales, traditional business ownership, and investing. And none of them can deliver on our Perfect Career List. So is the perfect career even possible? The answer is yes, but to get there you need to understand that everything is changing. The old models of compensation are dead or dying, and we are going through the biggest economic shift in any of our lifetimes.

The NEW Economy

The world as you know it has changed. For the people who don't recognize that fact, it will be the worst of times. For the people who do, it will be the best of times.

Over the last 100 years, an interesting phenomenon occurred. The rise of the corporation became the standard in society. The safe and respected place for people to exist in the workplace was as an employee.

Step one: Go to school to learn how to be an employee.

Step two: Find a company that will employ you.

Step three: Work for that company for 40 years.

Step four: Retire.

In recent decades, the promise of being rewarded by the company for your loyalty and hard work has been exposed as a myth. People began to realize the loyalty they were giving to their company was not being given in return. So a different process evolved.

Step one: Go to school to learn to be an employee.

Step two: Find a company that will employ you.

Step three: Switch companies for various political and economic reasons every three to five years over the course of your career.

Step four: Find that you can't retire comfortably after 40 years, so you keep working.

And now we are going through the biggest shift in any of our lifetimes. For a century, companies have paid people by the hour, by the week, or by the year. That's changing on a global level.

The world is moving toward a performance economy. And it's already happening. Here's what that means: In the future, you're only going to be paid for performance. You won't be paid for your time anymore. Servers in the food industry already live in this model. They get a very low hourly wage required by law and they make their living through tips, based on their performance.

If you can imagine the same model being applied to virtually every job in the world, you will see what is coming. The person cleaning the rooms in a hotel won't be paid by the hour anymore. They'll be paid per room.

For office workers, here's an example.

A person has a $60,000 annual salary.

Step one: The company will lower that salary to something like $50,000 because with today's marketplace there are other people to take the job for a lower amount.

Step two: They will reduce their "base" salary to something like $20,000 a year.

Step three: They will tell that person that they can get an additional $30,000 over the year if they hit certain performance benchmarks on a monthly basis.

In other words, if they hit their numbers, they can make an additional $2,500 a month. Now the pressure is on, and the company is loving it. If you don't hit your numbers they can save even more money. If you DO hit your numbers, guess what's in your future? They are going to raise your requirements.

Unless you are extremely specialized, this will happen to you if it hasn't already. Count on it. And it will happen in every single profession worldwide. The evolution has begun.

Why is this happening? One, it's a better model for the company. They'll get better results with less expense. Two, the New Economy needs fewer people, so the company has more people competing for fewer and fewer jobs.

Let me explain why the New Economy needs fewer people. The exponential rise of technology has changed everything. Over 100 years ago, 90% of the population worked in agriculture. Today, because of dramatic efficiencies, it's less than 1%, and the farming jobs are gone.

Remember customer service call centers where you talked to people? Today, you talk to a machine and those jobs are gone. Remember when companies had a massive amount of salespeople? Now people order online and those sales jobs are gone. Remember Blockbuster video and all of its employees? Now people watch movies on their handheld or tablet devices, and those jobs are gone. I love books, but go to your local bookstore while you can. They will be history soon, and so will the jobs provided by those stores.

I could go on and on through virtually every work category in the world. Technology and efficiency are eliminating jobs every single day, and there is nothing we can do to stop it. In fact, it's only going to accelerate. If you are sitting there waiting for the economy to bounce back and for jobs to return, don't. They aren't coming back.

Just like the children of farmers saw the handwriting on the wall and left farming for new vocations, the same thing is happening for people working in Old Economy jobs. To survive, they'll need to open their eyes to this reality and find something new.

Network Marketing is BETTER

The best way I know to not only survive, but to thrive in the New Economy, is Network Marketing. There are important products and services in the world today that need to be promoted to the people who need them. Consumers still need to be educated.

Companies have choices. They can dive into the ever-fragmented world of advertising to get the word out, they can hire a large and expensive sales force to sell their products or services, or they can utilize Network Marketing to tell their story to the world.

More and more companies will choose to use Network Marketing because it fits the New Economy. They can provide all the corporate support and pay distributors on a purely performance basis to promote their products. It's extremely efficient because in the New Economy, word-of-mouth advertising continues to work better than any other form of promotion. The company can just take the money they would have spent on advertising and promotion and pay it to their distributors to spread the word.

What that means for you as an entrepreneur is that you can receive all the benefits of traditional business ownership without the typical risks. And there will be no cap on your income, because Network Marketing companies WANT you to make as much as possible. If you're going to be paid for performance anyway, why live with the cap?

The "Catch" To Network Marketing

This all sounds great and it is. But there is a catch that most people won't tell you. Here it is:

You must accept a temporary loss of social esteem from ignorant people.

That means for a while, people still living in and trying to function in the old system will think less of you. They won't understand. They'll think you're crazy for being involved in Network Marketing.

And actually, the word "accept" isn't completely accurate. You need to do more than that. You need to embrace the temporary loss of social esteem from ignorant people. YOU are seeing the future before it becomes apparent to everyone else. YOU are the smart one. YOU are the person taking action to live a better life.

There is a reason why people will think less of you, and it's not just because they are stuck in the old system. Let me see if I can help you better understand this, because if you decide to make Network Marketing your profession, it's important to know.

Most people have either joined a Network Marketing company or know someone who has. This is what goes through the mind of virtually every person who decides to get involved. "Hmm, I can think of five or six people who might do this too! My sister would be great! My friend loves this kind of thing. I know this other person who could be amazing! Okay, I'll join."

In other words, they aren't joining a profession. They're just hoping to get lucky, sign up a few people to cover their own start-up costs, and sit back and wait for the money to roll in. The allure of being paid for someone else's efforts is powerful, but often badly misunderstood.

They haven't started a real business. They just purchased a glorified lottery ticket. Imagine a lottery ticket with six scratch-off spots. Those spots represent each of the people the new person thinks will certainly join. They approach those people and try to get them to join. And because of their lack of skill, most of them end up with nothing—just like the lottery ticket. This becomes just another lost opportunity, and since they have acted in unskilled ignorance, they may have damaged some friendships as well.

So they rip up the ticket, and instead of taking responsibility for not really starting their business, they blame Network Marketing and make sure to tell the world, "Look, I've been there. I've done it. I talked to every person I know, and Network Marketing just doesn't work. Save your money."

THAT'S what you're dealing with if you choose this as a profession—the opinions of ignorant people who think they've done it right and it doesn't work. If that's going to be too hard to handle, then Network Marketing isn't for you. But if you can embrace it, the world is yours.

The people who embrace this get paid BIG money. Companies will pay unlimited amounts to people who can help blind people see, who can educate the ignorant, and who can build a community of like-minded people.

Some people like to say, "Perception is reality." I hate that saying. All great leaders in the world have ignored it for centuries. What if Nelson Mandela had said perception is reality? What if Martin Luther King Jr. had said perception is reality? What if Steve Jobs had said perception is reality? The great leaders of the world said, "Reality is reality, and I'm going to do everything possible to help people understand that fact."

The truth is, Network Marketing isn't perfect. It's just BETTER. And that's reality!

CHAPTER TWO

If You're Going to be Involved in Network Marketing, Decide to be a Professional. Decide to Go Pro.

There are three categories of people in Network Marketing. I've seen all of them and I've been all of them. They are the Posers, the Amateurs, and the Professionals.

POSERS

Posers treat this profession as a lottery ticket. They're hoping to hit it big with as little effort as possible. When I first started out, I was a Poser, hoping to ride on my dad and his partner's coattails. Luckily for me, I got some results and that kept me going, at least in the short-term. But I think you can agree with me that remaining in the Poser category is a bad idea. Within about 90 days I moved out of that category and became an Amateur.

AMATEURS

Amateurs focus on different things. One of the things I continued to focus on as an amateur was luck. I was really hoping to get lucky and sign that monster distributor who was going to make me rich. We've all heard the stories of some person who had their lives completely changed by one sign-up. In reality, even if some of those stories are true, it really doesn't serve our profession very well, because it makes people spend their time hoping for that big hit.

The second thing I focused on as an amateur was timing. I was always worried about timing. Did I get in early enough? Could I be the youngest top-level person in the company? How many other leaders were already in my local market? Were there too many to compete against? Were there enough to get true momentum? How was the company? Was it too big? Did I miss the growth curve? Was it too small? I was obsessed with the idea of timing.

The third thing I focused on as an amateur was positioning. Was I in the right organization? Did other people have a better position than me? Maybe I didn't have the right upline. Would I do better somewhere else?

And the fourth thing I focused on as an amateur was short-cuts. I was always looking for an angle. Any gimmick that came down the road, I was up for it. Newspaper advertising? Okay. Help wanted signs by the side of the road? Let's go do it. Passing out fliers at the mall? I'm in. Going door to door? Let's try it. The Internet didn't exist when I was an amateur. Just imagine how crazy I would have been over all the Internet tactics I could have used to distract myself. What that meant was, every time I heard of some shiny new approach being trained by anyone in the world, I was digging into it to try to find the shortcut.

And then, I finally made the decision to Go Pro. Wikipedia's definition of a professional is, "A person who is paid to undertake a specialized set of tasks and to complete them for a fee." My definition of a Network Marketing Professional is, "A person who is an expert at the skills required to build a large and successful Network Marketing organization."

There is a phrase in our profession that does more harm than good. It says, "Ignorance on fire is better than knowledge on ice." The point of this phrase is that it's better to be excited and ignorant than it is to be apathetic and smart. That may be true, but why do we have to choose one or the other?

Let me give you an example. Let's say you were in need of an operation. At the hospital you meet your doctor. He comes in and says, "I'm very excited to conduct your operation. I'm so passionate about it I could hardly sleep. No one on earth wants to help you more than I do." You say, "Wow, thanks Doctor. How long have you been doing these type of operations?" And he says, "Well, I've never had any schooling on this particular operation, and I've never practiced and I've never done one, but it doesn't matter because I'm so passionate!" How are you going to feel? Enthusiasm is great, but eventually you need to marry that passion with skill.

Professional athletes will devote endless hours to preparing for competition but when they join Network Marketing, they won't give one day's worth of effort to learning our skills. Doctors will devote a decade of their lives at huge financial expense to become physicians, but when they join Network Marketing they won't give a month's study and practice to become a Network Marketing Pro.

In his book *Outliers*, Malcolm Gladwell's research showed it takes approximately 10,000 hours of practice to reach the expert level at anything. With four hours a day of practice, that adds up to about seven years. That formula applies to Network Marketing as well. It's going to take about seven years for you to become world-class. The good news is, the profession is very forgiving and you can earn a lot of money while you're becoming an expert. The trick is not to get complacent; don't stop learning while you're earning.

When I made the decision to Go Pro, everything changed for me. I stopped focusing on luck, timing, positioning, and shortcuts. I even stopped focusing on the money. My world changed when I started focusing on the skills and made the commitment to practice, practice, practice, until I mastered them.

Another thing happened when I decided to Go Pro. All of a sudden, my group started to grow. It was like people could sense my change of focus and my commitment to excellence and they wanted to be a part of it. Think about a time in your life when you were around a person committed to excellence. It might have been a teacher, a coach, a boss or a friend. How did it make you feel? It was inspiring, right? You'll find you will be an inspiration to others when you make this important shift.

Bottom line: If you're going to be involved in this great profession, decide to do it right and treat it like a profession. If you Go Pro, this business is great. If you stay a Poser or an Amateur, you're going to be miserable.

And by now, you've noticed I use the word profession a lot. I do that on purpose. Network Marketing is more than just a project. It's not an industry. It's a profession. If you do it right, it's truly a career choice. It can take you out of working in a job that doesn't make you happy to a place of total freedom.

That's why I called my website NetworkMarketingPro.com. Here's what I tell people every day: "Ladies and gentlemen, my wish for you is that you decide to become a Network Marketing Professional—that you decide to Go Pro, because it is a stone-cold fact that we have a better way. Now let's go tell the world."

When the site launched on March 11, 2009, very few people called themselves Network Marketing Professionals. That's no longer the case. Millions of people have changed the way they think about our business, and I'm proud of that fact.

I look forward to the day when it's common for people to hear:

> *I'm a doctor, but I'm also a Network Marketing Professional.*

> *I work in construction, but I'm also a Network Marketing Professional.*

> *I'm an athlete, but I'm also a Network Marketing Professional.*

The more people hear those words, the more the world will be ready for *a better way.*

CHAPTER THREE

Like Any Profession, You'll Need to Learn Some Skills

I hope by now I've been successful at convincing you that Network Marketing is a better way. I hope I've also gotten the point across that, if you're going to be involved, it's best to become a professional. The next step is recognizing that you'll need to learn some skills. But before we get to those skills, let me give you some good news.

Unlike most professions, you're not going to need a lot of money for your education. You won't have to take out student loans and you can actually earn while you are learning. In addition, this profession isn't biased. In fact, it's the most equal opportunity on earth. Your background, experience, contacts, age, race, or gender aren't going to be factors in your ability to learn the skills to Go Pro.

And finally, this isn't complicated. The skills necessary to grow a large and successful business are extremely learnable, and you'll have a surprising number of people financially motivated to help you learn them.

There are three primary elements to your Network Marketing business.

1 First, you have the company's products. If some people are successful in marketing those products and you're not, it isn't the product's fault. In other words, everyone in your company has the same products to offer to the public.

2 Second, you have the company's compensation plan. If some people are making a lot of money and you're not, it isn't the compensation plan's fault. There isn't one plan for men and one for women. There isn't one plan for different age groups, or educational backgrounds, or for the color of your skin. The compensation plan is the same for everyone.

3 The third element is the most important, and that element is YOU. You are really the only variable. Everyone has the same product and the same compensation plan, but you are going to be the difference between success and failure.

That means right here and right now, you need to take full responsibility for your Network Marketing business. Decide today never to blame anyone or anything else for your lack of results.

In fact, in Network Marketing there is something of an epidemic going on. People just love to blame their upline (the people above them in the structure) for all of their problems. "If my upline did this for me or did that for me, everything would be better."

If you're committed to building a large and successful organization, I'd like to encourage you to do something important. I'd like you to say goodbye to your upline. Call them up and say something like:

"I want to thank you for this opportunity. I appreciate it. Getting into business for myself was important and I appreciate you introducing me to a company that you believe in and that I now believe in as well. But from now on, when it comes to building my business, I will use you as a resource but never as an excuse. I may call on you from time to time. If you're available, that's great. If you're not, that's okay too. I'm going to build my business and I understand one thing: It begins and ends with me."

Everything changes when you take full responsibility for your Network Marketing career.

Would it surprise you to know there are only seven fundamental skills necessary to build a huge business in Network Marketing? Seven, not 70. Each one is fairly basic, but it always amazes me how little effort people put into learning them. If a college course were to be offered on Network Marketing, it would be one of the easiest classes to take. It's not rocket science but you'll be happy to know it's one of the highest paid skill sets in the world.

Let's explore each of them together.

CHAPTER FOUR

Skill #1—
Finding Prospects

Whehen people look at Network Marketing, one of their biggest questions is, "Do I know anybody? They believe if they know a lot of people, they can have lots of success, and if they don't know a lot of people, they don't have a chance. It sounds logical, but it's just not true.

As I mentioned in chapter two, there are three kinds of people in Network Marketing: posers, amateurs, and professionals. When it comes to finding prospects, the posers make a mental list of three, four, or five people they hope will join their business, and their entire future is based upon the response of those few people. If they're lucky enough to get one of them, they can extend the life of their career for a short time. They might even make another mental list of three or four people. Hopefully, they'll eventually decide to stop being a poser and upgrade to the amateur ranks.

Would it surprise you to know that approximately 80% of all the people who join Network Marketing approach the task of building a business as posers? It's true. Eight out of 10 distributors first approach their business with the poser mentality. They make a small mental list and see what happens. They never set out to develop the necessary skills. Your job is to make sure you're not one of them and to help your team do the same. Educate people. Help them understand how powerful this opportunity can be if they treat it with respect. For the posers, their only real chance is luck, and that luck had better happen fast.

The second group is the amateurs. Instead of a small mental list, these people make a written list, which is a step in the right direction. Let's say they make a list of 100 prospects. They charge out there with excitement, but not a lot of skill. They begin prospecting, and their list begins to diminish. As it grows smaller and smaller, their anxiety level grows higher and higher. Their biggest fear is running out of people to talk to. I know that was my biggest fear.

In my early 20s, my list wasn't anything to brag about. As I mentioned before, I tried to use my parents' contacts at the beginning, and it didn't take long for me to run out of names. Soon everyone in my world knew what I was doing and had either said yes or no. It was scary. I felt like if I didn't find some great people from my list and find them soon, I was going to fail in this business.

It never occurred to me that finding quality people to prospect was a skill. Up to this point in my new career, I always viewed "the list" as the ticket to wealth. If you had a good list, you'd succeed, and if you had a bad one, you either had to get lucky or you'd fail.

When I came to my defining moment and committed to become a professional, I began to study the people who had built large and successful organizations. I found that the professionals approached finding people to talk to as one of their core skills. It was part of their job to find new people. They weren't interested in luck. They weren't worried about running out of people. They developed the skill to make sure that never happened. The professionals started with a written list. But then they made the focused commitment to never stop adding to the list. They created something called an "Active Candidate List," and I'm going to show you how to do the same thing.

One of the people who taught me how to do this well was Harvey Mackay, author of the huge bestselling book *How to Swim with the Sharks Without Being Eaten Alive*. Harvey is a good friend and he's also one of the best networkers in the world. I once asked him how he built such a large and influential list of friends. He told me that at the age of 18, his father sat him down and said, "Harvey, starting today and for the rest of your life, I want you to take every person you meet, get their contact information, and find a creative way to stay in touch." He's done that for over 60 years, and today his list of friends totals more than 12,000 people. And these aren't just social media friends. They're real friends, and I consider myself fortunate to be one of them.

If you want to master this skill, follow these four simple steps:

1 **Step one:** Make your list as comprehensive as possible. Include every person you can think of. EVERY person. It doesn't matter if you think they are a prospect or not. Your database will be one of your most important assets. Everyone goes on the list. If they are negative, put them on your list. If you hate them, put them on your list. If they are your best friend, put them on your list. If they've said, "I'll never be involved in Network Marketing," put them on your list. If they're 98 years old, put them on your list. If they're 18 years old, put them on your list.

It's important to do this, because as you empty your mind out on paper, it will make more room for new contacts to find room in there. When you write down your nephew, you will begin to think about the circle of people around your nephew. All of these connections will become apparent to you as you make your list more and more comprehensive. Think about everything—every organization you've ever been involved in, every group you've ever been a part of, everything you've ever done. If you do this right, it will end up being hundreds and hundreds and maybe even thousands of people.

You're not required to prospect everyone on your list. That's up to you. But it's extremely important to do the work necessary to truly capture your network on paper.

Step two: Have you heard of the concept that we're all only six contacts away from any person in the world? Six degrees of separation? I'm not sure if that's a myth or if it's true, but I believe in the concept. Step two is looking at your list and thinking about the people they know—the second degree of separation. Chances are, you'll know most of them also.

Think about members of your family. Who do they know? Add them to your list. Think about your friends. Who do they know? Add them to your list. Think about all the relationships in your life. Who do they know? Add them to your list. Don't worry about what you're going to do with this list yet. We'll talk about that a bit later. Just keep building it.

3 **Step three:** Constantly expand your list. This is why the professionals call this an "Active Candidate List." It never stops growing. The pros have a goal to add at least two people to their list every single day. They may not prospect them, but as Harvey Mackay's father said, they go on the list and you should find a creative way to stay in touch. Harvey's book *Dig Your Well Before You're Thirsty* deals with this concept. If you think about this as a core skill, you'll realize it isn't very hard. You come into contact with people every day. Just add them to your list. You meet people through online social media. Add them to your list. You do business with new people. Add them to your list.

My friend Jordan Adler is the author of *Beach Money*®, and he's also a seven-figure-a-year earner in Network Marketing. He's a master at step three. He just lives his life and is always making new friends, and if you look at his business, almost all of the people he's recruited into his huge organization are people he didn't know before he started his Network Marketing business. He's a Pro.

Professionals develop a higher level of awareness. They pay attention to the world. They know they will be introduced to new people all the time. Posers and amateurs don't even notice. They just go through their day saying "What people? I don't see any people."

How hard would it be to raise your awareness and add two new people a day to your list? Think about it. If you did that six days a week, that is over 600 new people a year. Do that for five years and it's over 3,000 people. Can you see why professionals don't worry about running out of people to talk to?

Please understand, I'm NOT saying you should assault these people with your pitch the moment you are introduced. Some people in Network Marketing make that mistake and it's not good. Just add them to your list, make friends, develop a connection, and when the time is right you can help them understand what you have to offer.

4 **Step four:** Network on purpose. Professionals network on purpose. It's hard to meet new people if you're hiding from the world. Get out there. Have some fun. Join a new gym. Have fun with a new hobby. Volunteer for a cause that's important to you. Find places and organizations where you can meet new people. Not only will it be good for your business, but you'll also make some great friends.

CHAPTER FIVE

Skill #2— Inviting Prospects to Understand Your Product or Opportunity

O nce you've identified your prospects, the next skill is learning how to properly invite them to find out more about your product or opportunity. This is by far the most critical skill to develop. I call it the "gateway" skill for Network Marketing. If you aren't successful in getting anybody to take a look, then we can guess what your future will look like in MLM.

Most people think you must start off with a great reputation and have a lot of influence with others for them to take a look at your opportunity. That's just not true. When I first started in 1988, I had no reputation and no influence. I barely escaped high school, attended one semester of community college before dropping out, and had a total of 18 jobs—all before the age of 23. Do you think I had a lot of respect in the community? I had zero. And since I was a $5 to $10 an hour person, all my friends were the same so they weren't much help. Most of them were still living with their parents.

But I was desperate and I was scrappy. In the beginning, I made up in numbers what I lacked in skill. I called everyone I knew and gave them my pitch. A few of them joined. Most didn't. I placed ads in the local newspaper. I gave all of the people who responded my pitch. From all of that activity, a few joined. Most didn't.

I tried everything. I was like a hunter with the goal of bagging an elephant. I went around with a gun/opportunity in my hand and shot at everything that moved. I didn't really care about relationships. All I cared about was getting that new recruit. My attitude was, "Some will. Some won't. So what? Next!"

But because I was a hunter, everyone around me felt hunted. And they started to avoid me. And it wasn't fun. Even worse, the people I did get to join my business tried to do the same thing I was doing, failed, and then quit.

After three or four years of frustration, I came to my defining moment, and started studying successful people in MLM to see what they did. What I found surprised me. They weren't hunters. They were more like farmers. They built relationships. They built friendships. They learned how to build trust with the people they met and were able to skillfully transfer the belief they had about their products and opportunity. Their goal wasn't to immediately recruit their prospects. Their initial objective was to educate their prospects on what they had to offer and then let those prospects decide if it was something they wanted to do.

This was a HUGE switch in strategy for me and I began to look at things differently. I put myself in the prospect's shoes and thought about what would be attractive to me and alternatively, what would cause me to put up my defenses. I realized why the pros had such great results. Instead of acting like sharks, they were more like coaches or consultants. They built relationships and then offered common-sense solutions to people's problems. Who wouldn't like that?

The other thing I noticed with the professionals is they didn't "pitch" their product or opportunity. Instead, when the timing was appropriate, they just invited people to do one of two things, based upon the individual prospect's situation.

The first thing they did was to invite people to attend some sort of event, such as a one-on-one or two-on-two meeting with another member of their team, a three-way phone conversation, a small group presentation in their home, an online webinar, a local hotel meeting, or some larger company event or convention. Professionals understand that personal interaction is a critical component when it comes to building trust and transferring belief, so they try to connect with people as much as possible.

The second thing they did was to invite people to review some sort of tool. I'm a BIG believer in using tools to help educate a prospect. Tools take many forms. There are CDs, DVDs, magazines, brochures, websites, and online presentations. With some companies, you can even let people sample the product and treat that as a tool.

There is no question that technology continues to evolve, offering more and more convenient ways to help educate prospects, but I have to interject a personal opinion based on experience. While technology allows us to get people quality information quickly, there is nothing like a physical tool. In a world of bits and bytes, and in a Network Marketing world where it's important to build trust, a physical tool makes it real.

Of the two methods used to help educate the prospect, events are the most effective. There are lots of reasons. There is physical interaction from meeting with people, and that helps build trust. There is the important element of "social proof". It's valuable for the prospect to see that there are other people actively involved, and find out what those people are like. There is education on the product and the financial opportunity. They get to see first-hand the kind of support that's involved and they realize they won't have to do everything by themselves. In most cases, there is excitement and urgency at these events. And, they get to hear stories of how things are going for other people.

Those are some of the benefits. The only downside to events is they can be difficult to schedule and confirm, especially for a brand new person. If you don't have the skills, it's fairly common to invite twenty people and have only one or two show up. That can be discouraging.

For building a large and duplicating organization, I have found that a tool is a better first step. Remember, our goal is education and understanding. We want people to know what we have and understand how it can benefit their lives. A tool is a great way for people to become educated (and hopefully excited) in the middle of their busy lives. They might not have time to drive across town to meet with you, but they could listen to a CD in their car, watch a short DVD, read a magazine, or watch an online presentation.

If you were to look back at my career, you'd see that tools changed everything for me. In 1990 my company came out with a video that was dynamic and exciting. Even though it was wildly expensive at $15 each, back then it was worth it, because when you learned how to invite people to watch that video, the results were dramatic.

Everyone in the company became focused on a daily method of operation that centered around inviting people to watch our video. We allowed no distractions. Our entire culture revolved around this strategy and our growth went through the roof. Events were still very important, but they were a second step after a person watched our video.

By adopting this new approach, my organization finally broke out, and I was able to enjoy the experience of having a group that grew with or without me. It was more fun than I can describe. My group grew from a few dozen to a few hundred and then to a few thousand. All I did was learn how to successfully invite people to watch a video, follow it up with an invitation to an event, and teach everyone else to do the same thing.

The second career breakthrough took the form of an audiocassette. Yes, I said cassette. This was 1992 and that's all we had. The company was launching something new and exciting, and this time I personally recorded an audio that explained the opportunity in detail. We sold it for 50 cents apiece, which covered our costs, and in less than one year, that little audiocassette sold over a million copies. We taught people how to invite prospects to take that cassette, put it in their car, and listen to it right away. The results were amazing.

We trained people to get 100 cassettes at first, get them out to everyone they knew, and then had them focus on getting out two-a-day after that. Using that simple system, my income grew to almost $1 million a year.

Different companies use different tools and event strategies to grow their business. Some use home parties. Some use online presentations. Some use one-on-ones with magazines and flip charts. Find what's working best in your particular company, develop your daily method of operation, and then train your people how to effectively do the same and invite their prospects to plug in.

As a professional, you are going to be inviting your prospects to review a tool or attend an event. Here's what you're NOT going to be doing: You're NOT going to be pitching people and trying to dazzle the world with your wisdom. That approach will feed your ego but steal from your bank account.

Let me give you my formula for financial independence in Network Marketing.

> *Your ability to get a large group of people to consistently do a few simple things over an extended period of time.*

It was this formula that helped me break out of Network Marketing mediocrity, and it will help you do the same.

For years, I focused and depended on my ability to persuade people to join me. Then I graduated to finding a few key leaders I could train to do what I was doing. And finally, I learned the formula I just gave you and began to focus on getting a large group of people to consistently do just a few simple things and to keep doing them. When that happened, everything changed for the better.

Those are the fundamentals. Let's take a moment to talk about the emotions of inviting. There are four basic rules.

Rule Number One

You must emotionally detach yourself from the outcome. This is extremely important. Remember, our initial goal is education and understanding. It's not getting a new customer or signing a new distributor. In other words, if you disconnect your emotions from that outcome and just focus on education and understanding, everything gets very simple.

This sounds easy, but it's difficult to do. All of us come into this business with the hope of recruiting some great people. It's hard to disconnect from those expectations. But you need to remember, we're not hunters. We're not sharks. Our job is to educate people and help them understand what we have to offer. We act as consultants offering suggestions on how people can live a better life.

If you focus on getting a customer or new distributor, you'll constantly be disappointed and you'll find your prospects running away from you.

If you focus on education and understanding, you'll have fun and your prospects will enjoy the experience.

Rule Number Two

Be yourself. So many people become a different person when they start inviting. This makes everyone uncomfortable. Be yourself. Just focus on being your best self.

Rule Number Three

Bring some passion. Enthusiasm is contagious. It's okay to get a little bit fired up. Get focused. Listen to some music that inspires you. Smile when you're on the phone. I assure you, your positive emotion will translate into better results.

Rule Number Four

Have a strong posture. This was a big one for me. At first I was so insecure. I didn't think anyone would take me seriously. But as I watched the professionals, I noticed their posture. They were bold. They were confident. They were strong.

So I decided to be bold as well. I stopped apologizing all the time. Instead of saying, "Yes, I know I've had a lot of jobs so far in my life, but I'm hoping this will be the change I've been looking for," I started saying "Guess what? I'm sick and tired of the life I've led up until this point and I've decided to take charge. I wouldn't bet against me because I'm serious." Do you feel the difference?

Be yourself, but be a bolder self. Be yourself, but be a stronger self. Be yourself, but be a more confident self—at least when you're inviting. I found I could do that for short periods of time at the beginning and, just like building a new muscle, I could eventually do it longer and longer until it became a part of me.

So now that we've set the stage, let's go through the invitation formula. This formula is designed to be used over the phone or face to face. It's NOT to be used with texting, email, or any other communication tool—just on the phone or face to face. This can work with your warm market prospect (someone you know) or cold market prospects (someone you meet while living your life). I'll give you examples for both.

There are eight steps to a professional invitation. That might sound complicated, but with a little practice, you'll find it's an easy skill to master.

Step One: Be in a hurry

Step Two: Compliment the prospect

Step Three: Make the invitation

Step Four: If I, would you?

Step Five: Confirmation #1–Get the time commitment

Step Six: Confirmation #2–Confirm the time commitment

Step Seven: Confirmation #3–Schedule the next call

Step Eight: Get off the phone

Step One: Be in a hurry

This is a psychological issue. People are always more attracted to a person who has things going on. If you start every call or face-to-face conversation giving the impression that you're in a hurry, you'll find your invitations will be shorter, there will be fewer questions, less resistance, and people will be more respectful of you and your time.

Examples for warm-market prospects:

"I don't have a lot of time to talk, but it was really important I reach you."

"I have a million things going on, but I'm glad I caught you."

"I'm running out the door, but I needed to talk to you real quick."

Examples for cold-market prospects:

"Now isn't the time to get into this and I have to go, but…"

"I have to run, but…"

Get the message? Set the tone with some urgency.

As for the examples I'm sharing with you, don't worry too much about the exact words. Just focus on the concept and use your own words. Let people know you're busy, you've got a lot going on and your time is short, but it was important for you to talk with them real quick. And do it with some passion in your voice.

Step Two: Compliment the prospect

This is critical. The sincere compliment (and it must be sincere) opens the door to real communication and will make the prospect much more agreeable about hearing what you have to say.

Examples for warm-market prospects:

"You've been very successful and I've always respected the way you've done business."

"You've always been supportive of me and I appreciate that so much." (Great to use with family and close friends.)

"You have an amazing mind for business and can see things other people don't see."

"For as long as I've known you, I've thought you were the best at what you do."

Examples for cold-market prospects:

"You've given me some of the best service I've ever received."

"You are super sharp. Can I ask what you do for a living?"

"You've made this a fantastic experience."

The key to the compliment is, it must be sincere. Find something you can honestly use to compliment your prospect and use it. This simple step will literally double your invitation results. When you start with urgency and a compliment, it becomes very difficult for a person to react negatively to your invitation. People don't hear compliments very often. It feels good. You will find your prospects will become very receptive.

If you study the pros, you'll find they are constantly putting people in a good mood through their honest and sincere compliments. It helps to build rapport, it helps to open people's minds, and mostly, it helps achieve our goal of education and understanding.

Step Three: Make the invitation

This is a situation where one size does NOT fit all. There are three kinds of invitation approaches for the Network Marketing Professional.

The Direct Approach

This is used when you are inviting people to learn more about an opportunity for THEM. Most people use a Direct Approach for all of their prospects. It usually goes something like this: "I found a way for you to get rich! Let me tell you all about it. Blah, blah, blah." I understand the passion, but really, who's going to get excited about that, unless they're getting a call from a millionaire?

That doesn't mean the Direct Approach doesn't work. It does. It has an important place in your invitation process. But it should be reserved for people who know and respect you or for people that you know are searching for something better.

Examples for warm-market prospects:

"When you told me you (hate your job, need more money, wanted to find a new house, etc.), were you serious or were you just kidding around? (They'll almost always tell you they were serious.) Great! I think I've found a way for you to (get it/solve the problem/ make that happen)." This is for situations where you know an area of their dissatisfaction, need or desire.

"I think I've found a way for us to really boost our cash flow."

"When I thought of people who could make an absolute fortune with a business I've found, I thought of you."

"Are you still looking for a job (or a different job)? I found a way for both of us to start a great business without all the risks."

"Let me ask you a question, off the record. If there was a business you could start working part-time from your home that could replace your full-time income, would that interest you?"

Examples for cold-market prospects:

"Have you ever thought of diversifying your income?"

"Do you keep your career options open?"

"Do you plan on doing what you're doing now for the rest of your career?"

You can follow these cold market scripts or any variation with the following: "I have something that might interest you. Now's not the time to get into it but..."

The Indirect Approach

This is another powerful tool to help get people past their initial resistance and educate them on what you have to offer. The Indirect Approach is about asking the prospect for help, input or guidance. I used this approach extensively and with great success when I first started out. Because of my lack of credibility at age 23, I couldn't get much success with a Direct Approach, so I learned to play myself down and play up to the prospect's ego. It worked incredibly well and it still works today.

Examples for warm-market prospects:

"I've just started a new business and I'm really nervous. Before I get going I need to practice on someone friendly. Would you mind if I practiced on you?" (This is a GREAT approach for family and close friends.)

"I found a business I'm really excited about, but what do I know? You have so much experience. Would you look at it for me if I made it easy on you and let me know if you think I'm making the right move?"

"A friend told me the best thing I could do when starting a business is to have people I respect take a look at it and give me some guidance. Would you be willing to do that for me if I made it simple?"

Examples for cold-market prospects:

When you meet someone from another city, state, or country, and if your company does business there, you can say:

"My company is expanding in your area. Would you do me a favor and take a look at it and let me know if you think it would work where you live?"

When you meet someone who might provide good input on your product, you can say:

"I've started a business with a product I think makes a lot of sense, but I'd like to get your input. Would you be willing to check it out and give me your opinion?"

The Super Indirect Approach

The third approach is the Super Indirect Approach. This approach is incredibly powerful because it works on a number of psychological levels. In this approach, you tell the prospect they aren't a prospect and you're just interested in finding out if they know someone else who might benefit from your business. It's very effective.

Examples for warm-market prospects:

"The business I'm in clearly isn't for you, but I wanted to ask, who do you know that is ambitious, money-motivated, and would be excited about the idea of adding more cash flow to their lives?"

"Who do you know that might be looking for a strong business they could run from their home?"

"Who do you know that has hit a wall with their business and might be looking for a way to diversify their income?"

"I work with a company that's expanding in this area and I'm looking for some sharp people that might be interested in some additional cash flow. Do you know anyone who might fit that description?"

In most cases, they're going to ask you for more information before they give you any names (behind that request will be curiosity and intrigue, thinking this might be for them, but they're not going to admit that to you yet).

When they ask for more information, you can respond with:

> "That makes sense. You'll want to know more about it before you refer some of your contacts." Then you can just move to step four.

Examples for cold-market prospects:

Cold market is exactly the same as warm market for the Super Indirect Approach. Just use the warm-market scripts or any variation that's comfortable for you.

Step Four: If I, Would You?

This question has been my secret weapon for a very long time. It is by far the most powerful phrase I've come across in building a large and successful Network Marketing business.

"**If I** gave you a DVD, **would you** watch it?"

"**If I** gave you a CD, **would you** listen to it?"

"**If I** gave you a magazine (or some other printed material) **would you** read it?"

"**If I** gave you a link to a website with a complete presentation, **would you** check it out?"

"**If I** invited you to a special invitation only webinar, **would you** attend?"

"**If I** invited you to a special invitation-only conference call, **would you** listen in?"

This question is SO POWERFUL, and for a number of reasons.

First, it's reciprocal. You're saying you will do something if they will do something. As human beings, we are hardwired to respond positively to these types of situations.

Second, it puts you in a place of power. You're in control. You're not begging. You're not asking for favors. You are simply offering a value exchange.

And third, it implies that YOU have something of value to offer. You're saying you will do something, but not unless the other person will do something in exchange. When you value what you have, people will respect you.

When I first started, I didn't know about this magical question. I just said things like, "I really, really, really, want you to watch my video, try my product, listen to this CD, etc." You can imagine the results. The whole psychology of it is weak. If you use, "If I, would you," you're having a business conversation. If you use, "I really, really, really, want you," now you sound desperate, and a desperate distributor is NOT attractive. If you've used this approach you already know what I'm talking about.

"If I, would you," gets results. It gets people to say "yes." It helps prospects see what we have in a different light. Remember, our goal is education and understanding. "If I, would you," helps us achieve that goal.

If you've started the call with urgency, complimented the prospect, made the invitation and asked, "If I, would you," their answer will be "yes" almost 100% of the time, and you can just go to step five.

If they ask for more information first, just respond with, "I understand you want more information, but everything you're looking for is on the (DVD, CD, printed piece, link, etc.). The fastest way for you to really understand what I'm talking about will be for you to review that material. So, **if I** give it to you, **would you** review it?"

If they say no, then thank them for their time and move on. Also, review steps one through three to see what you might have done better. But do NOT give your material to them.

So you've gone through the first four steps and the person said yes! Success! They've agreed to review your tool! Does that mean they will follow through? Nope. In fact, only about

5% of your prospects will do what they said they would do if you just use the first four steps—and 5% is not a good number. To get closer to 80%, you need to complete the invitation process professionally.

Step Five: Confirmation #1–Get the time commitment

You've asked, "If I, would you," and they've said yes. The next step is to get a time commitment.

> "When do you think you could watch the DVD for sure?"

> "When do you think you could listen to the CD for sure?"

> "When do you think you could read the magazine for sure?"

> "When do you think you could watch the link for sure?"

Don't suggest a time for them. (That's another mistake I made early on in my career). Just ask the question and wait for them to respond. This question makes them think about their schedule and their commitments, find a place to review your tool, and communicate that back to you. In other words, it makes it real.

When you first asked, "If I, would you," and they said yes, it was someday. When you get the time commitment, it starts to be real. The only thing that matters is that they give you a time. It doesn't matter what that time is. Let them think about their schedule and tell you when they will have reviewed the materials for sure.

About 90% of the time, they'll give you an answer. The other 10% of the time, they'll be vague, saying something like, "I'll try to do it sometime." If they do that, then tell them, "I don't want to waste your time or mine. Why don't we just lock in a time when you'll have seen it for sure?" Remember, they already said they'd review it in step four. This is just confirming the time.

The key to all of this is they have now said yes twice—the first time when they answered, "If I, would you," and the second time when you received a time commitment from them.

So now you can give them the tool, right? Wrong. You're not done yet. The professionals take a few more seconds to complete a couple more steps before they're finished.

Step Six: Confirmation #2–Confirm the time commitment

If they tell you they'll watch the DVD by Tuesday night, your response should be something like, "So, if I called you Wednesday morning, you'll have seen it for sure, right?" If they say they'll listen to the CD by Thursday morning, your response should be, "So, if I called you sometime later in the day on Thursday, you'll have listened to it for sure, right?" If they say they'll watch the link by July 1, your response should be, "So, if I called you on July 2, you'll have looked at it for sure, right?"

They will either naturally say yes, or they will adjust the time slightly. In any case, the significance of step six is they've now confirmed three times and they are now much more likely to follow through—and,

> The key is, this isn't an appointment you've set. It's an appointment *they've* set.

They said they'd review the materials, they would do it by a specific time and, if you called them after that, they would have reviewed the materials. You've asked the questions. Their answers made the appointment.

Step Seven: Confirmation #3–Schedule the next call

This step is simple. Just ask, "What's the best number and time for me to call?" They'll give you what works best for them, and now you have a real appointment. All you have to do is be sure to remember to call when you said you'd call.

They've said *yes* four times. The whole invitation took a few minutes, and your chances of achieving your goal of education and understanding has gone from about 5% to about 80%.

Step Eight: Get off the phone

Remember, you're in a hurry, right? Once you've confirmed the appointment, the best thing to say to someone is something like "Great, we'll talk then. Gotta run!"

Too many people make the appointment and then un-make it by talking and talking and talking. Remember, our goal is education and understanding and we're going to let the third-party tool do most of the work.

Here are some examples of all eight steps:

A person you know who hates their job—Direct Approach

"Hey, I don't have a lot of time to talk, but it was really important I reach you. Listen, you're one of the most financially intelligent people I know and I've always respected that about you. When you told me you really didn't like your job, were you serious or were you just kidding around?" (They say they were serious.)

"Great, I think I've found a way for you to create an exit strategy. I have a CD that describes what I'm talking about better than I can. If I gave you this CD, would you listen to it?" (They say yes.)

"When do you think you could listen to it for sure?" (They say Tuesday.) "So if I called you Wednesday morning, you'll have reviewed it for sure, right?" (They say yes.)

"All right, I'll check back with you then. What's the best number and time for me to call?" (They give the information.)

"Got it. We'll talk then. Gotta run and thanks!"

A good friend—Indirect Approach

"Hey, I'm running out the door, but I needed to talk to you real quick. Do you have a second? Great. Listen, you've always been so supportive of me and I appreciate that so much.

"I've just started a new business and I'm really nervous. Before I get going I need to practice on someone friendly. Would you mind if I practiced on you?" (They say sure.)

"Great! If I gave you a DVD that laid out the information in a professional way, would you watch it?" (They say yes.)

"It's about 15 minutes long. When do you think you could watch it for sure?" (They say Thursday.)

"So if I called you Friday morning, you'll have reviewed it for sure, right? Fantastic, what's the best number and time for me to call?" (They give the information.)

"Great, we'll talk then. Gotta run and thanks!"

A highly successful person—Super Indirect Approach

"I know you're busy and I have a million things going on too, but I'm glad I caught you. You've been wildly successful and I've always respected the way you've done business.

"I've recently started something new and I'm looking for some sharp people. It's clearly not for you, but I wanted to ask, who do you know who is ambitious, money motivated and would be excited about the idea of adding a significant amount of cash flow to their lives?" (They say they do know some people.)

"I understand that you'd want to know more about it before you recommend people. I have a DVD that explains exactly what I'm doing and the kind of people I'm looking for. It's brief.

"If I sent one to you, would you review it? (They say they would.) "Thanks. When do you think you could view it for sure?" (They say next Monday.)

"Okay, so if I called you next Tuesday, you'll have reviewed for sure, right?"

"Okay, I'll check back with you then. What's the best number and time for me to call?" (They give the information.) "Okay, great. Thanks again, I appreciate it so much. Talk to you next Tuesday."

A cold-market prospect who's done a good job selling you some something—Direct Approach.

"Now isn't the time to get into this and I have to go, but you are super sharp and I happen to be looking for some sharp people. Do you plan on doing what you're doing now for the rest of your career?" (They say no.)

"Good. I have something that might interest you. Now isn't the time to get into it, but I have a DVD that explains it all in great detail. If I gave it to you, would you watch it?" (They say yes.) "When do you think you could watch it for sure?" (They say Sunday.)

"So if I called you Monday, you'll have reviewed it for sure, right?" (They say yes.) "All right, I'll check back with you then. What's the best number and time for me to call?" (They give you their information.)

"Okay, here it is. Thanks again for the excellent service and I'll talk to you soon."

Are you feeling the flow of how this works? Obviously there are many possible variations for different kinds of prospects, but I hope these examples help you understand how everything comes together.

In terms of scripts, it's best if you get the basic concepts down and don't focus too hard on the exact script. Life doesn't work that way. But if you learn to let your prospect know you're in a hurry, then compliment them, then invite them, then pass on a tool with, "If I, would you," then confirm using the process I described, and finally get off the phone or complete the invite, you'll do just fine.

Remember, in recruiting, there are no good or bad experiences—just learning experiences. On your journey to becoming a Network Marketing Professional, the best thing that can happen is for you to develop the skills to recruit on demand, in any situation. Then you never have to worry about being lucky. So practice, practice, practice.

CHAPTER SIX

Skill #3—
Presenting Your Product
or Opportunity to Your
Prospects

We've talked about the first two skills of identifying prospects and inviting them to learn more about your product or opportunity. As you've learned, you'll be inviting them to review a tool or attend some sort of event.

If they are reviewing a tool by themselves and you're not around, there's nothing for you to do. Just follow up when you said you would. If you're physically with them, there are some things you need to understand, and one of the biggest is, YOU are not the issue!

This was a tough one for me to accept. When I first got started, I read everything I could, listened to everything I could, and attended all the training sessions I could. I thought the most important thing I could do was become an expert on all the facts associated with my company so if anyone asked me any questions, I'd be right there with the answers. Sounds logical, right?

I would sit down with someone and say, "Let ME tell you all about our products. Let ME tell you all about our company. Let ME tell you all about our compensation plan. Let ME tell you all about our incredible support system." There are big problems with that approach if you want to build a large and successful organization. For me, the first problem was, no matter how much I learned, there would still be questions that stumped me. And since I was presenting myself as the expert, if I got stumped, that might make the prospect question the whole opportunity.

The second problem was, most of my prospects knew I wasn't an expert. So when I came to them and presented myself as an authority figure, they knew it wasn't true. It actually made them more skeptical.

The third problem was, even if I was successful at becoming an expert, the other distributors in my organization didn't necessarily have that same desire or willingness to learn. As a result, I was the go-to guy for every single presentation. There's no way to create an organization that will duplicate with this approach, and without duplication, Network Marketing is just a job.

In the early days, that's what Network Marketing was for me—a job. I had no duplication because I made myself the issue. But I was determined and I started to observe and take careful note of how the most successful distributors did their presentations.

The pros never made themselves the issue. More than that, they never presented themselves as an expert. They acted as a consultant who connected the prospect to tools, events, or other distributors to help them become educated. If the prospect asked a question, they would guide them to the answer, but they wouldn't give the answer directly. This baffled me until I started to comprehend duplication. The pros knew they could sign the person up by dazzling them with their knowledge and experience, but they also knew it would take a long time for their new distributor to do the same, so they came up with a simpler approach.

It was around this time I heard a concept that has stuck with me ever since:

> In Network Marketing, it doesn't matter what works. It only matters what duplicates.

This should be a guiding principle for every Network Marketing Professional.

The pros use tools instead of their own wisdom. The pros use live events instead of their own presentations. The pros use other distributors to give the facts instead of giving them themselves. The pros don't present themselves as experts; they just invite people to learn more about the product or opportunity and let the third-party resource provide the information. The pros bring passion, enthusiasm, excitement, and belief. If you ever watch a pro at work, you'll see a fire in them that is contagious. Make passion, enthusiasm, excitement, and belief your priority, then invite professionally and let the third-party resource do the rest.

In addition to learning how to effectively present your product or opportunity during your personal recruiting efforts, it's also important to learn how to present your opportunity to groups of people.

I've heard it said (and I think it's true), "The person with the marker makes the money." In other words, the person in front of the room giving the presentation usually has a higher than average income. When I first got started I was deathly afraid of speaking in front of people, but I was ambitious, and since everyone said this was an important skill, I was determined to master it.

I started by learning how to give a short and effective testimonial. Learning to tell my story was extremely valuable in building my business and has been to this day. People aren't interested in how much you know, but they ARE interested in your story, as long as you don't bore them to death with it.

I worked on my story for a while and, after tweaking it a time or two, here is what I came up with. "Hi! My name is Eric Worre and I'm a retired underachiever. I had 18 jobs by the age of 23 and was starting to think my future wasn't looking so good. I was embarrassed by my lack of results and I was desperately looking for a way to make something of my life. In January of 1988, I was introduced to Network Marketing and it has changed my life. Instead of being afraid of the future, now I'm excited about it." (And then I would insert whatever was appropriate based upon my current levels of success.)

The theme of my story was, if I could do it, anyone could do it. And it worked. I used it all the time. In hotel meetings, in home meetings, on three-way phone calls, on conference calls—you name it.

No matter what your background is, you can craft a compelling personal story. I've found every good story has four elements:

1. Your background.

2. The things you didn't like about your background.

3. How Network Marketing or your company came to the rescue.

4. Your results, or how you feel about your future.

Take some time to create your story and start telling it every chance you get.

Next I decided to master my company's opportunity presentation. Again, the concept of modeling successful people came into play. The top earner in my company was extremely powerful and effective. In addition, he did the same exact presentation every single time, just about word for word. So I recorded his presentation and transcribed it by hand onto a legal pad. When I completed that step, I recorded my own voice doing that presentation. I did it word for word. Same stories, same jokes—everything was his exact presentation.

After I was done, I played it back and it was terrible! My voice had no energy. I was boring. I hated it. So I recorded it again and again and again until it was acceptable. In the end I had an audiocassette with my presentation on it, and I listened to it over and over in my car. I'll bet I listened to that presentation 500 times, and by that time, I had it memorized. I knew it backward and forward. I could start from any part of the presentation and take it from there.

You would not believe the confidence this gave me. I went from being afraid to do the presentation to actively looking for opportunities to give it! I did the presentation on conference calls, in home meetings, on three-way calls, and any place else I could find. I became a regular presenter at our local meetings and continued to move up to bigger and better venues, even being asked to speak at company conventions.

For me, the evolution of becoming a presenter went through several stages:

1. Learning my story.

2. Learning the standard opportunity presentation.

3. Learning different training presentations.

One big defining moment as a presenter came in 1993. I was 29 years old and starting to make a name for myself in Network Marketing. I was having a conversation with the CEO of the company and the number one distributor at the time. I can't remember exactly how the topic came up, but I recall saying something to the CEO like, "Well, he (the top distributor) might be a better networker than I am right now, but I can out-speak him anytime."

It was meant as a joke, but the CEO raised his eyebrows and said, "Okay son, I'll tell you what. We have our big convention coming up. Over 14,000 people will be in attendance. I'll give you both the same amount of time and we'll have a private contest. I'll handpick a few judges and they will vote on who did a better job."

Wow! Now I was really on the hook! I wasn't a huge leader. I didn't have as big an organization or reputation at the time as the top earner. So, I did the only thing I could control. I started to prepare like my life hung in the balance. I chose a theme. I wrote my talk and rewrote it over and over. I did research. I practiced. I recorded myself doing the speech. I did everything I could possibly do.

When the day came, I'd never felt so nervous in my entire life. Talking to 14,000 people is like talking to an ocean. But my preparation served me well. I steadied my 29-year-old insecure self and delivered.

The response was overwhelming! The crowd went wild, literally. I felt a little numb when I walked off stage as they were still cheering, and sat there while the top earner gave his speech. He did a fine job, but I have to admit to you, it felt so good to have the CEO come up and congratulate me for winning our private little contest. It was definitely a defining moment.

That speech was lost for a very long time but a copy was recently discovered. If you'd like to hear it, you can do so by going to this link:

www.networkmarketingpro.com/calltoaction

My voice sounds quite a bit younger, but it's still me.

To summarize this skill set, remember a few important things:

1 When you are prospecting, you are the messenger—not the message. Get yourself out of the way and use a third-party tool.

2 Learn to tell your story in a way that will make your prospects curious to hear more.

3 When it comes to presenting in front of a group of people, preparation is key. When you're prepared, it's fun.

CHAPTER SEVEN

Skill #4—
Following Up With Your
Prospects

In MLM, they say the fortune is in the follow-up. I think that's true, because most people in MLM don't follow up at all, at least not as professionals. You need to understand some important concepts if you're going to master this skill.

Concept #1–Follow-up is doing what you said you would do.

If you say you're going to call at a specific time, then do it. The Network Marketing Profession is full of people who get all excited one minute and then go missing in action the next. Run your business through a physical or electronic calendar. Be the person who does what they say they're going to do. People will respect that.

I sold real estate the year before I got involved in Network Marketing. My father and his partner owned the company. One day I was in the office and a gentleman by the name of Chuck Aycock showed up for a 10 a.m. meeting with my dad. It was 9:55 a.m. and my dad wasn't in the office yet. I greeted Chuck and told him I was sure my dad would arrive soon. At 10 a.m. exactly, Chuck got up and said, "It's 10 o'clock. Your dad isn't here. Have him call me if he wants to reschedule the meeting."

I couldn't believe it. He came all the way to the office just to leave 30 seconds after the appointment? I told him, "Mr. Aycock, I'm sure he'll be here any minute. There's no need to leave."

And then he told me something I never forgot. He said, "Son, either you are early or you are late. He's late and my time is valuable. Have him give me a call if he'd like to reschedule." And he left!

My dad showed up at 10:10 a.m. expecting to meet Chuck. I told him what happened and he was as stunned as I was. My dad wasn't habitually late or anything. That particular morning he was just a little casual with his time. He rescheduled the appointment and I noticed over the years that my dad was ALWAYS early for his appointments with Mr. Aycock.

What is the lesson in this story? For me, the lesson was that people respect a person who does what they say they're going to do. People also respect a person who values their own time. If you say you're going to follow up at a specific time or in a specific way, either do it or reschedule well ahead of your appointment.

Concept #2–The only reason to have an exposure is to set up the next exposure

When I got started, I would conclude every exposure by saying, "What do you think?" No one told me that was one of the worst things to do. It felt like a natural thing to say, but my results were terrible.

I asked one of my early mentors for help and he said, "Eric, the only reason to have an exposure is to set up the next exposure."

That blew my mind. I thought the reason to have the exposure was to get the person signed up! He went on to explain that if you finish each exposure by setting up the next one, the prospect will eventually become educated on the opportunity and make an informed decision.

The goal in my mind changed from "getting" the prospect on the first exposure to just keeping the process alive by setting up the next follow-up exposure, then the next and the next, until they made a decision. When I made this small improvement, my results improved dramatically.

We talked earlier about how to professionally invite your prospect to take a look at what you have to offer. At the end of that process, we went through several steps to set up the NEXT exposure, meaning your follow-up call. That was your next appointment.

When you make that call, you're going to ask them if they reviewed the material. They'll say, "No, I didn't," or they'll say, "Yes, I did." Let's talk about how you'll set up the next exposure in both cases.

If they say no, they didn't have a chance to review the materials, it's important you don't show your displeasure at their lack of follow-through. It sounds funny, but a lot of people just jump on their prospects with, "I thought you said you'd be able to see it for sure!" Obviously, this won't help build that good relationship you're working on.

The best way to respond is, "That's okay. I understand sometimes life gets busy. When do you think you could do it for sure, for sure?" Now, you might say "for sure, for sure" is a little much, but I've used that for decades in this follow-up situation, and I do it because it works. In any case, use whatever language you'd like to use to set up the next time and walk through the same steps to get the commitment. Once you have it, including the date and time of the next call (the next exposure), then hang up and call them when you said you would.

If you call them at the scheduled time and they still haven't reviewed the material, just repeat the process until they do. Remember, they are setting the appointment and you are being the professional by following up like you said you would.

If you call your prospect and they say yes, they've reviewed the material, you're going to ask them a few intelligent questions. First, you're NOT going to ask, "What did you think?" This just invites the critical part of the prospect's mind to come up with objections to try to sound smart.

The best follow-up question I've ever used is, "What did you like best?" This question will take you in a very positive direction and will give you clues as to the level of their interest. If they say "the product," then your next exposure will probably be product-related. If they say "financial freedom," then your next exposure will be opportunity-related.

Another great question to ask is "On a scale of one to 10, with one being zero interest and 10 being ready to get started right away, where are you right now?" With this question, anything over a one is GOOD. It says they have some interest. Most of the time you'll get something like a five or a six. No matter what number they give you, all you're going to do is ask them how you can help them get to a higher number. Usually that answer will go along the lines of how they answered, "What did you like best?"

If the answer is very positive and the number is fairly high, you can go directly into the closing process (we'll cover that in the next section). If it isn't an obvious green light, then you'll just schedule the next exposure.

They might want to try the product, so you help them do that, and set a follow-up date—a time to call them and check on the experience (the next exposure). They might want to understand the compensation plan, so you set up a time to get together and review it (the next exposure). They might want to talk with their spouse, so you send them home with materials they can share with their spouse and set up a date and time when you'll follow up (the next exposure). Whatever it is, you never finish one exposure without setting up the next one. Never! If you do, it's over.

That's what used to happen to me at the beginning. I would have someone look at the opportunity. When they'd done that, I'd say, "So, what do you think?" They'd usually mumble something like, "I'll let you know," or, "I'll get back to you," or, "I need to think more about it," or something similar. And poof, they were gone. Then, when I tried to call them back, I was just bothering them. The whole thing felt uncomfortable.

Once I changed to never finishing one exposure before setting up the next one, everything changed for the better. I was being professional. I was in control. The prospect had more respect for me and for the opportunity. All of this happened from this one small change in mindset.

Concept #3–It takes an average of four to six exposures for the average person to join

When people don't understand that the only reason for an exposure is to set up the next exposure, they put too much pressure on their prospects and on themselves. In the "some will, some won't, so what, next" MLM culture, people hammer on a person once, and if they don't join right away, they move on and never follow up. In many cases, they take it a step further by damaging the relationship with the prospect with their attitude.

Professionals understand that it takes an average of four to six exposures for a prospect to become involved. Their goal is education and understanding. It's hard to educate someone in one exposure. So they take them from exposure to exposure to exposure, knowing it will eventually sink in. Through that process, they also build a stronger relationship with the prospect. They strengthen the friendship. That helps build trust, and people enjoy working with people they like.

Four to six exposures is an average, which means that for every person who joins on the first exposure, there's going to be a person who takes more than 10 exposures to join. You just never know. Some of the best people in Network Marketing were prospected for years before they finally made the decision to take part in the opportunity.

Keep your urgency—but have patience.

Concept #4–Condense the exposures
for better results

Posers prospect someone once and move on. Amateurs prospect someone through several exposures over time. Professionals condense those exposures into the shortest time possible.

People are busy. They are constantly distracted by life. When you are approaching them to take a look at something new, it's important to keep their interest; the best way to do that is to stack the exposures as close together as possible.

If you go slow, you might start by having them check out a video. Then a few weeks later, have them listen to a conference call. Then a month later, have them attend a webinar. Then after another month, invite them to a three-way phone call with you and another distributor. This slow process is difficult because between each exposure they tend to get distracted by life. It can almost be like starting over every time.

On the other hand, if you have them check out a video, then join a conference call, then try the product, then get on a webinar, then participate in a three -way call, then come to a live meeting (or whatever combination of exposures you use in your company), and do it all in one week, you give them the opportunity to really think about how this could change their lives.

Questions and Objections

At every step in the recruiting process, you'll come across questions and objections. This is natural. A lot of the time, your prospect will just be bringing them up to sound intelligent. They don't want to seem easy, so they throw out objections to feel better. How you respond is extremely important. If you act defensive, you'll plant a seed of doubt in their minds. If you act offensive, you'll chase them away.

Remember, our goal is education and understanding. It's not to win an argument. Our job is to help blind people see. When someone brings up a negative question or if they offer you an objection, all they are really doing is helping you to identify one of their blind spots. It's helpful to know what these are so you can assist your prospects in eliminating them.

I'm going to give you some specific tactics to help overcome objections, but the thing I want you to remember and spend more time focusing on are concepts. Tactics come and go. Concepts are timeless.

> **I've found that objections fall into one of two categories. The first is the prospects' limiting belief in their abilities. They aren't sure they can be successful. The second is a limiting belief in Network Marketing. They aren't sure Network Marketing will help them achieve their goals in life.**

For both categories, one of the best concepts is empathy—how you relate to people. And the best way I know to relate to people is to let them know you're just like they are. You had the same doubts, the same questions, the same fears, and you overcame them. Believe it or not, your story (and the stories of others) will do more for you in overcoming objections than anything else.

There's an old tactic called "Feel/Felt/Found." It works with the concept of empathy. When a prospect offers an objection, you respond with, "I know how you feel. I felt the same way. But here is what I found." You can use that quite literally and with great success. You can also modify it based upon your story and your prospect.

When Prospects Have a Limiting Belief in Their Abilities

The common objections in this category are:

"I don't have the money," "I don't have the time," "It's not my thing," "I'm not a salesperson," "I don't know anyone," or "I'm too old/too young/have no experience."

Some people teach fancy approaches where you make yourself seem smart and the prospect seem stupid.

"You don't have the money? Do you have a cable bill? Do you have a cell phone? Do you ever go out to dinner? You have lots of money. C'mon, wake up!"

Or,

"You don't have the time? How long do you want to have that reality in your life? You have to change if you want your life to change!"

How does it feel when you read that? How would it feel if someone were to say it to you? Pretty bad, right? A better approach is to relate to the person and tell your story.

When a person tells me, "I just don't have the money right now," I respond, "I had the same exact challenge. I didn't have enough money to pay my bills, let alone start a new business. But when I thought about it, I realized if I didn't have enough money to pay my bills now, how was I going to change that in the future? I was tired of being behind. I was tired of always scrambling. I wanted more out of life. So you know what I did? I found a way, and it was the best decision I ever made. Let me ask you something... if you really felt this was a chance for you to take control of your financial future, do you think you could find a way to make it happen?"

Nine times out of 10 they would agree they could find a way. Again, forget the exact words and focus on the concept. I told them I was the same as they were, with the same objection. I told them about my pain. And I told them I found a way to solve it. As a result, we bonded. We related to each other. We were in the same boat with the same hopes and dreams.

And if I didn't have a personal story that would compare with theirs, I would tell another person's story. There are plenty of stories inside your company that can relate to virtually every situation. So when a prospect tells you their objection, you can say, "I know what you mean. I have a friend who had that same exact problem and let me tell you their story."

Can you see how that approach would work with all the objections based on a person's limiting beliefs about themselves and their lives? The concept is simple, it's proven, and the results are amazing.

When People Have Limiting Beliefs About Network Marketing

This category includes:

"Is this MLM?"

"Is this one of those things?"

"Is this a pyramid scheme?"

"I'm not interested in MLM."

"I don't want to bother my friends," and,

"How much are you making?"

Let's start with the one that strikes fear into the hearts of most people in our profession—"Is this MLM?" or variations like, "Is this one of those things?" or, "Is this a pyramid scheme?" or, "I'm not interested in MLM."

Some people go a little crazy when they hear this question. They say, "Pyramid scheme? Like every corporation in the world? Like the government? You mean like THAT?!"

Instead of going crazy on your prospects, it's important to understand where this question comes from. My experience has shown me that they usually knew someone who joined with no success or else they've done it themselves (usually they just purchased a virtual lottery ticket like I described earlier and it didn't pay off). This scenario represents well over 90% of the people who will ask this kind of question. The rest of them have heard of opportunities like this and are rightfully skeptical of the promise of getting rich quick.

If they ask this kind of question with any sort of emotion, I know they've been involved at some point, so I say, "Wait a minute. You have a story. What happened? Were you involved in Network Marketing at some point?" Then just let them tell you their story. It opens them up. It lowers their defenses. And it allows you to ask some questions about their experience.

Let me give you a typical example. I'm going through my invitation process when the prospect says, "Wait a minute. Is this MLM?" And they say it with emotion. I reply, "Oh, you have a story. Did you try it out at some point? What happened?"

They say, "Yeah, I joined a company a few years ago, bought some product and lost my money." I reply, "What do you think was the reason you didn't have success?"

They say, "Well, my friend talked me into it. I didn't have a lot of time and I thought more people would join right away but they didn't. I guess I just lost interest." I reply, "Do you think you really gave it a fair shot?"

They say "No, not really." I reply, "Do you think Network Marketing was the problem? Or do you think maybe your timing wasn't right?" They say, "It was probably the timing."

Do you see the dynamic? I've had thousands of these conversations and they're all slightly different, but if you ask some questions and are friendly through the process, you have a strong opportunity to help them get rid of their blind spot and take a look at what you have to offer.

In addition, you can relate to them by saying you had the same objection initially and telling them how you overcame it. If someone uses the word "pyramid" with me, I always say, "Oh no. Pyramid schemes are illegal, and I would never be involved with something illegal."

For people asking without the emotion attached, I usually respond with, "Yes, this is Network Marketing. Do you know anything about it?" Again, I'm asking questions and waiting for answers. From those answers, I ask more questions, and through the process I can achieve my goal of education and understanding.

"I don't want to bother my friends," is slightly different. Again, I relate to them by telling my story or someone else's story. And then I ask questions like, "What makes you think you'd be bothering your friends?" or, "If you truly believed in the product, would you let your friends know about it?" and, "If I could show you how we share this product with others without it feeling or sounding like a sales pitch, would that help you?"

The last in this category is, "How much are YOU making?" If you are making money already, this is a great question. If you're not, your answer depends on how long you've been involved. If you're brand new, you can tell them you're just getting started. If you've been around for a while and not making big money yet, you can tell them you are working this part-time and are really excited about your future. You could also say that you're excited about your future with this company because you knew things weren't going to change if you didn't do something to change them.

The other way to answer it is to tell your story and then tell stories of people you know who ARE making good money. You can even suggest setting up a phone conversation with those people so they can feel more comfortable about the opportunity.

All of this takes practice, but if you get the concepts down, you'll find it becomes easy. And the other thing that should encourage you is you'll only have this handful of the same objections for the rest of your career. There's nothing new here. What I've listed in this section is about all there is. Remember, our goal is education and understanding. This is a part of the process that makes that goal a reality.

CHAPTER EIGHT

Skill #5—
Helping Your Prospects
Become Customers or
Distributors

This skill is a natural byproduct of following up professionally. As you walk through exposure after exposure, our goal of education and understanding will be accomplished. But that doesn't mean the prospect will come out and ask you for an order form or an application. It's your job to guide them to a decision.

The key to success in this area is a combination of having good posture and asking good questions. Good posture means the way you carry yourself. Your words and actions will help your prospect feel more confident about joining your opportunity or they will plant seeds of doubt.

In my early years, my posture was terrible. I was trying to "get" people instead of pursuing the nobler goal of education and understanding, and the prospects could feel my intentions. I was very emotionally attached to the outcome. You could even say I was needy. Every time I got to this part of the process, I really, really wanted it. Again, the prospect could feel my emotional attachment and that usually scared them away.

Through lack of results and without even realizing it, I started to assume people were not going to be interested. And that assumption started to seep into everything, which led to the predictable result of the prospect not joining.

Most of the time I wasn't properly prepared. I didn't have applications, start-up materials, or whatever else was necessary. Think about the subconscious impact this had on my prospects. It seemed like just about everything I did projected a lack of belief and a lack of professionalism.

Instead of asking questions and listening intently to the answers, I just talked and talked and talked. I was more focused on being interesting than being interested. Prospects don't like that. No one does.

So, again I followed my pattern of modeling the professionals. I watched what the best closers did and began to copy them. I interviewed top performers to figure out what they did differently. And slowly, I started to see the flaws in my approach.

First, I learned that professionals are emotionally detached from the outcome. In other words, their goal is education and understanding while helping a prospect make a decision that would positively impact their life. They are the opposite of needy. They aren't trying to "get" anybody. They are honestly just trying to help.

Second, they are very assumptive in their approach. They expect the person to join because their belief that the opportunity would benefit the prospect is so strong. They are rock solid. Many of them are sincerely shocked when a person decides not to get involved.

Third, it was interesting to learn they promote themselves as much as they promote the product or opportunity. What I mean by that is they help the prospect make the decision by saying, "You get ME!" When they promote themselves, it isn't like, "I'm going to do everything for you." It was more like, "We have a great product and a great opportunity, but I'm going to take this thing to the top and we can do it together." This gives people great comfort in knowing that they don't have to learn everything on their own.

Fourth, they are always prepared. Always. They have everything they need to get a person started right on the spot.

And fifth, they ask question after question after question and are great listeners. They act like a consultant helping a person with a problem. The best consultants in the world have to ask a bunch of questions before they can offer a solution. Network Marketing Professionals use questions as their most powerful tool.

As you can imagine, it took me a while to figure all of this out and that was just half the battle. It's one thing to have the information and it's another thing to put it into action. I wasn't as talented as the pros, but I could model what they did, so I just started to act like they acted.

I acted emotionally detached (I really wasn't at the beginning); I started to act very assumptive that people would join (I really wasn't at the beginning); I started to tell people, "and you get ME!" (even though I didn't think that was such a huge benefit at the beginning); I was always prepared; I started asking lots of questions, focusing more on being interested than interesting.

And as time went on, I acted less and less, and believed more and more. The same can happen for you.

Let's talk about questions. If you were a consultant and your job was to figure out if an opportunity was a good fit for your client, what would you do? You'd ask questions right?

In working to help a prospect make a positive decision about your opportunity, you're going to do the same thing. But instead of asking, "What did you think?"—which leads nowhere—learn to ask questions that lead in a positive direction.

"Did it make sense to you?"

"What did you like best about what you just saw?"

"Pretty exciting, isn't it?"

"Can you see how this could be an opportunity for you?"

Of these examples, the one I use the most is, "What did you like best?" The answer to that question is almost always positive and it gives you clues as to the area in which they are most interested.

Then I like to say, "Let me ask you a question. On a scale of 1 to 10, with one meaning you have zero interest and 10 being you're ready to get started right now, where are you?" They will give you a number. And it's usually obvious from their number that they either need more information before they will make a decision or they are leaning toward getting started now.

If you feel they need more information, just guide them to the next exposure that will help them the most. But if you feel they are ready to get started, then ask a series of four questions. This "Four Question Close" has produced strong and consistent results over the course of my career. If you learn it and use it, you'll be amazed at how many people you can help.

Question #1: "Based on what you've just seen, if you were to get started with this company on a part-time basis, approximately how much would you need to earn per month in order to make this worth your time?" Instead of asking this question, most distributors say things like, "How would you like to make $10,000 a month?" Don't do that. Instead of prescribing what you think they want, just ask them what it would take to make it worth their time and wait for their answer.

Question #2: "Approximately how many hours could you commit each week to develop that kind of income?" Now they have to go inside their head and check their mental calendar to see how much time they would invest to get that kind of money.

Question #3: "How many months would you work those kind of hours in order to develop that kind of income?" This question makes them think about their level of commitment if they want the income from question #1.

Question #4: "If I could show you how to develop an income of (their answer to question #1) per month, working (their answer to question #2) hours a week over the course of (their answer to question #3) months, would you be ready to get started?" Most of the time, you'll get a positive answer to this question. And when people say, "Sure, show me how," you can pull out your compensation plan and sketch out a reasonable game plan to achieve their goals.

There are rare occasions when people give you unrealistic numbers. They might say they want $10,000 a month working two hours a week for one month. It doesn't happen often, but it does happen. If you face that situation, you act as a consultant and say, "I'm sorry, but your expectations are way too high. You can get to $10,000 a month but it will take more hours and more months than you're willing to commit. If you're willing to change those expectations, we can talk."

If you don't get a positive answer to the four questions, that's okay. It just means the prospect will need to have more exposures before they're ready. Schedule the next one and repeat this process when you're done. This skill will take practice. But it's a skill that will serve you for the rest of your career. If you're tired of having too many people thinking about it and not enough taking action, this will help.

CHAPTER NINE

Skill #6—Helping Your New Distributor Get Started Right

In Network Marketing, people invest enormous effort, time and money into getting people signed up, and then squander that investment by leaving their new distributors to figure everything out for themselves. Professionals don't do that. They set proper expectations, they help get some quick results, and then continue to guide the new distributor through the many phases of our profession.

I was lucky enough to have an early mentor, Michael Nelson, who was very skilled at guiding new distributors. Michael wasn't in my upline, but he was clearly the leader in my city. In addition, he had a lot of experience in our profession. So I listened to what he said, I watched what he did, and I asked him tons of questions.

Back in those days, he had a small office close to my home, and I was always hanging around trying to learn something. Michael was a very successful recruiter. He was always bringing on new people. And for the most part, Michael's people did well in the business. That wasn't happening for me. The few people I recruited did nothing.

As I watched Michael, I noticed that every time he signed up a new distributor, he scheduled what he called a "Game Plan Interview." I decided to model what he did. So the next time he met with a new distributor, I sat behind them, close enough to take notes on their conversation. I did this several times, and was surprised to learn he went through the same exact interview every time. I thought if I could learn that interview process, then I'd have a chance at his results.

Game Plan Interview—Part One

He validated their decision to become a distributor. He said things like, "Congratulations on making the decision. I'm proud of you for taking charge of your life. From now on, things are going to be different for you and your family." It always took less than five minutes, but by the end of their discussion, any doubt they may have had about becoming a distributor was gone. They felt great.

Game Plan Interview—Part Two

He set their expectations. He knew most people came into our business with unrealistic expectations, so he always said the same three things:

"If you succeed in this business, it's going to be you who creates that success, not me. And, if you fail in this business, it's going to be you who creates that failure, not me. You are going to be the difference between success or failure. I'm here to guide you every step of the way, but I can't do it for you. I'm here to work with you, but not for you."

Wow, this was a radical concept and so different from the conversations I had when I got a person started! I said things like, "I get paid from what you produce, so I essentially work for you!"

Well, what kind of expectation do you think THAT set in the new distributor's mind? I'd also say, "WE are going to build a business together," when that wasn't really true. THEY needed to build a business. I could be a resource, but I couldn't do it for them.

The next thing he said was, "My job is to help you become independent from me as quickly as possible. Do you agree that's a good goal?"

Again this was radical, but it made sense. Up to that point, I had a group that was extremely dependent on me. They only did something when I pushed. But Michael had a group that produced on their own without his constant help. He had duplication and freedom. I didn't. This set the relationship up so Michael would be the teacher for his group and not the slave. He could show them the skills and then they could independently build from that point forward.

The third thing he said was, "There will certainly be ups and downs as you build your business. There will be good times and bad times. I'll know you're in one of the bad times when you aren't calling me, you aren't showing up for meetings, you aren't on the calls, if I start hearing excuses—that sort of thing. When that happens with you, and it happens with everyone, how do you want me to handle that? Do you want me to leave you alone or do you want me to be persistent and remind you why you made this decision in the first place?"

This was brilliant because it's true that everyone will have times of self-doubt. He let them know it was natural and at the same time, set up the relationship so he was in a position to turn them around when it happened.

What Michael accomplished with these three concepts was so different from promising the world like I was doing, that it was like night and day. With my approach, the distributor would sit back and wait for me to perform. And if I was ever too busy or couldn't help for some reason, I became the easy excuse for why things weren't working out. With Michael's approach, his people became independent quickly. He would coach them from time to time, but he wouldn't allow his group to use him as an excuse for their lack of results. While my distributors struggled, his flourished.

Game Plan Interview—Part Three

Michael went through a getting-started checklist to help the new person have the best chance for success. The exact plan would be different for every company, but the concept was to do everything possible to get quick results.

Here are some examples of what you could include in your getting-started checklist:

1 Make sure your new distributor is set up with appropriate products. Just about every company has products that can be personally used by the distributor, so make sure your new person is doing that. Depending on your company, this may include a monthly commitment. It's very important that people develop an emotional attachment to the products and that can only happen if they are using them and enjoying the benefits. In addition, many companies have products that can be sampled or used in demonstrations. In that case, new distributors should have an appropriate supply so they are properly prepared.

2 Make sure your new distributor is set up with appropriate tools. We've talked about the importance of third-party tools in building a large and successful Network Marketing business. Your new distributor needs to be prepared to help their prospects with the tools that will professionally take them through the exposure process.

3 Make sure your new distributor gets connected. Show them how to find things on the company website, where the upcoming events are being held, when the leadership calls or webinars are being conducted, etc. Remember, our goal is to help them become independent as quickly as possible. This is an important step in making that goal a reality.

4 Make sure your new distributor has a basic understanding of the compensation plan. They don't need to know it in detail at the beginning, but they should at least understand the key points and what will happen financially as they move through the first few levels.

5 Make sure your new distributor has a fundamental understanding of how to properly invite their prospects to understand more about what they have to offer. You can save them from running out there and talking their heads off with little or no results by giving them a brief overview of how and why a professional invitation process works.

Game Plan Interview—Part Four

Michael helped the new distributor create a game plan to get through the first few ranks and challenged them to do it quickly. He understood, and helped me to understand, that it was a race to help a person get results quickly. If they received early positive reinforcement, they'd continue. And if they didn't, they had a tendency to fade away.

Every company is different, so this game plan will also be different. But think about the simple actions you could encourage people to take during their first week to get the best possible results.

How can they get their first customer?

How can they get their first distributor?

Can you encourage them to attend their first company event?

What steps can you take to help them earn their first commission check?

Success in Network Marketing wasn't real for me until I earned that first check. When it arrived, everything changed for me. I started to really dream about creating a better life for myself and my family. Helping your new person get off to a quick start is vital.

Game Plan Interview—Part Five

Michael always ended by giving some specific assignments. One thing I've learned is new distributors crave direction and they respond incredibly well to simple assignments. Michael always ended by giving those assignments along with a deadline for them to be completed. He told his new distributor to get back to him by a specific date. It's just like the exposure prospecting process. You go from exposure to exposure, but it doesn't end when they become distributors. The professionals continue to go from exposure to exposure, assignment to assignment.

The purpose of all of this is to help the new distributor get "over the line." When someone gets started, there is always a line between success and failure. On one side of the line, it's easier to quit than to continue. On the other side of the line, it's easier to continue than to quit.

What can help a person get over the line?

- Signing up their first customer

- Signing up their first distributor

- Getting their first commission check

- Attending a big company event

- Making friends inside the organization

- Proclaiming their intentions to the world

- Getting promoted to a new level

- Being recognized for some sort of achievement

There are hundreds of other things that can contribute to a person getting over the line. As a sponsor, your job is to help them get over the line and STAY over the line. And the line never really goes away. It's always there and you, as a leader, need to be constantly aware of where your people are emotionally. This way you can continue to encourage them to never let go of their dreams.

CHAPTER TEN

Skill #7—
Promoting Events

In Network Marketing, meetings make money. It's just that simple. Yes, technology can help us connect with people in ways that are becoming more and more efficient, but nothing replaces face-to-face interaction.

Meeting people one on one, in small groups, or at local or bigger events, will have a huge impact on the long-term success of any Network Marketing organization. But one particular type of event is the most powerful, and that is the "destination" event. It might be a company-sponsored event or one put on by your upline leadership, but a "destination" event is one where most of the attendees travel to a different city, stay at a hotel, and participate in a conference or convention.

Some try to argue that the destination event is dead in the new technology world and people won't travel for these things anymore. All I can tell you is those people aren't top earners in our profession. If you study what the successful people do

111

to build their Network Marketing organizations, you will find that virtually every one of them uses destination events as a cornerstone for building their business.

There's something magical about getting away from your day-to-day grind and focusing completely on your dreams. Total immersion, even if it's only for a weekend, is GOOD. You can use it to refocus and recommit to your future and gather the strength necessary to go back home and do what's necessary to move your business forward.

You gain strength from the presentations you hear during the event. Sometimes a person says something at just the right time in your life, and it changes you forever. Over 20 years ago I was at a convention when a guy by the name of Johnny Daniel said, "You can tell the size of the man by the size of the problem that gets him down." That statement went right into my heart and has helped me ever since. If I ever get sad or depressed, something inside me says, "Is this the size of Eric?" I answer, "No," pick myself up, and get moving again.

I've had hundreds of those moments over the years at destination events. I gave up blaming at an event. I decided to become a professional at an event. I realized no one could stop me at an event. I decided to go to the top at an event. In fact, as I think back, I can't think of a single significant moment in my Network Marketing career that didn't happen at an event. They are that powerful.

In addition to gaining strength from the presenters, you also receive incredible validation of your decision to be involved. It's a concept called "social proof," and it's very important. As human beings, we're wired to seek proof from sources outside of our own thoughts and experiences. At a destination event, you see lots of other people who've made the same decision you have, and that feels good. Also, you see how some of them have overcome their fears and gone to the highest levels in your company. You start to think, "If they can do it, maybe I can do it too."

There's also some positive peer pressure involved. Most destination events include recognition programs—who won the contest, moved to the next rank, earned the top income, or spoke from the stage.

When I went to my first event and saw all the people walking across the stage, I had one thought: "The next time, I'll be walking across that stage." It was inspiring that so many people had accomplished what I hadn't done yet. It made me think I could do it and it made me work on a plan to make it happen. In addition to being inspired, I also didn't want to show up at the next event without some improvement in my business. That positive peer pressure helped me face my fears and make it happen.

Overall, the sense of community at a destination event is comforting. We all live in a world filled with ignorant people when it comes to Network Marketing. That can get discouraging at times. But when we go to a big event, suddenly we are surrounded by people who think like WE think. They have similar beliefs, hopes, dreams, aspirations, and positive attitudes. Spending time with this amazing group of people can literally fill us back up again so we have strength for the next push.

Once you understand how important destination events are to the success of your business, you need to learn how to effectively promote them to your organization. It's really very simple: The more people from your group attend events, the more money you're going to make in our profession. Top leaders know exactly how many people are attending and they make sure to grow that number at every new event.

Think about it. Take two distributors who each have a group of 100 people. Distributor A makes it a priority and gets everyone to attend every major destination event. Distributor B doesn't make it a priority, so only a handful attend. Which group is going to be more successful? It's not even a contest.

The first step in developing a culture that promotes attendance at destination events is to personally be more committed than anyone else to attending, and helping others make the same decision. That means you need to lead by example, and never miss a destination event.

When I first started in this profession I didn't know how I was going to do it. I didn't have the money and I couldn't afford the time; I had the same obstacles as anyone else. But something happened to me at my first event that changed everything. I scraped up enough money to get there and it was a mind-blowing experience: The stage, the lights, the people, the stories—it was awesome.

During one of the sessions, I stepped out to go to the bathroom and when I came back to the entrance to the big convention hall, I found myself standing next to one of the top income-earners in the whole company! It was like standing next to a celebrity. He had achieved what I wanted to achieve, and more. I stood there trying to think of something smart to say. Finally, I simply introduced myself and asked, "What's the secret?"

Today I know there isn't a secret and he could have said the same thing to me, but instead he had a little compassion and gave me an important lesson that serves me to this day. He said, "Eric, do you see this room? It holds about 2,000 people. We have these events about three times a year. Here's the secret. At the next event, half of these people won't come back, but the other half that does will be making about twice the average of everyone else in the room. Your job is to be in the 1,000 people who come back. And it doesn't stop there.

At the next event half of those 1,000 won't come back, but the 500 who do will be making four times the amount of the average in the room. This continues from event to event. If you continue to come back, you'll end up being among the highest paid people in the room, and eventually you'll even find yourself presenting on stage."

I said, "That's it?" And he replied, "Eric, obviously you're going to have to continue to work on your skills in between events, but my experience has shown me that if you outlast people at our big events, you'll make it to the top." This was pretty simple for me to understand. I thanked him and made a resolution on the spot to never miss a big company event.

It wasn't easy. Sometimes the event tickets alone were a problem. I made it a priority and found a way to buy them. Sometimes childcare was an issue. I relentlessly searched for babysitters until we found someone we could trust. Sometimes I struggled with how to get to the event. Instead of taking a nice comfortable direct flight, I sometimes had to book one with two or three connections. Instead of flying, sometimes I had to drive, even piling into one vehicle with a group of people to get there. There were even times when I reserved a bus and recruited people in my area to share the ride. The point is, I made it a priority and I made it to the event—no matter what.

As for accommodations, today I stay in a suite, but it wasn't always that way. At the beginning I often shared a room with as many people as possible. Instead of room service, we would go to the local grocery store and get food for inexpensive meals. And the minibar was strictly off limits.

Bottom line, the advice I received all those years ago WORKED. Because I was ambitious and hungry, I figured out a way to outlast the people who were less committed and, just like that top income-earner had told me, my income continued to grow with each event.

On top of that, another strange thing happened. I started to feel different than everyone else. I started to feel like an "Iron Man." I started to be proud of the fact that I was still standing when other people lost faith. So, if you're more committed than anyone else to attending the destination events, that all-important commitment will serve you very well.

Once you are fully committed, the next step is to grow the number of people on your team that attend with you. Most people announce the next big event to their group, sit back, and hope people register. Professionals understand there is a big difference between being an "announcer" and being a "promoter."

Promoters make the event a priority in their group. They are relentless with their message. They tell stories that inspire people to action. They take nothing for granted and don't rest until people have registered. They paint a picture in people's minds about how great the event will be and the benefits of attending. One thing I learned long ago was to never buy someone's excuse, at least at the beginning. I can't tell you how many people started off by telling me the reasons they couldn't attend the next destination event, only to find out their reason was just an excuse, and wasn't really true.

The problem with amateurs is they buy that first story and that's the end of it. A person says, "I can't get off work," or, "I can't afford it," or, "I can't arrange childcare," or, "Who's going to watch my dog?" or, "There's a birthday party that weekend." And the amateur says, "Oh well, it is what it is. I hope you can make it to the next one."

The professional has a completely different mindset. When they hear an objection, they don't buy that story be-cause they know it's probably not real—or at least not real enough. Instead they work with that person to help them un-derstand the meaning and importance of attending the event. Then they brainstorm with them to figure out a way to over-come their initial problem. I can't tell you how many people I've talked to who had already decided they weren't going to attend the next event, and within five minutes, they'd changed their mind and registered. The lesson here is to tell your story. Don't buy theirs.

Think of this skill as if you are a publicly traded company and your stock value is tied directly to how many people you have at each destination event. If that were the case, you'd make it a priority to always have a bigger number at the next event, wouldn't you? You might start with just you at the first event, but then the goal needs to be to bring some people with you to the next one, and to grow that number at the next and the next and the next. There's no such thing as a silver bullet in Network Marketing, but this skill is as close as it gets.

CHAPTER ELEVEN

Anything Worthwhile Takes Time

If a person starts a traditional business, they expect to break even in their first few years and possibly pay back their initial investment in the first five years. But when a person starts a Network Marketing business, they expect to get their money back in the first month, make a profit in second month, and get rich by the third month. And when that doesn't happen, they blame Network Marketing!

It's like people don't want the laws of the business world to apply to Network Marketing. We DO have a better way, but we're not selling magic beans here. Anything of value takes time to develop.

I learned a great lesson early in my Network Marketing career: From time to time in your life, your income might take a lucky jump. You might be in the right place at the right time. But if you don't quickly grow as a person to that new higher level, your income is going to come back down to the level of who you really are. In the end, you only get to make what you are.

How many people do you know that hit it big and lost it all? I learned this lesson the hard way in my first few months in MLM. Back in 1988, I joined a company that had a $5,000 upfront package, which paid the sponsor between $1,200 and $2,400, depending upon their level. Although I'm glad most of those big money packages have left our profession, back then a person could make some pretty big money fast.

In my first month with that company, I earned approximately $7,400! If you remember, my strategy was to quickly call my dad's friends before he could get to them. I was ecstatic! In my second month, I earned about $12,200. Unbelievable! But then reality kicked in. I wasn't a $12,000 a month person. I hadn't worked on my skills. I wasn't developing myself. I was just riding the wave. My third month's check was $1,098.60. Looking at that check was like looking at myself in the mirror. It showed me who I was. It was an ugly feeling.

My first reaction was to quit and blame everyone and everything for my bad check. But eventually I realized that to earn more, I needed to become more. I needed to work on my skills so I didn't have to rely on luck or timing or positioning.

> You might have heard, "You can get rich quick," or, "There's no work involved," or, "The product sells itself," or any number of trumped up statements. But you must learn to give up those false and unrealistic expectations and go to work on YOU.

The 1/3/5/7 Formula

There's a formula I've seen work in our profession. I call it the 1/3/5/7 Formula. As a general rule, it will take you about one year to become competent and profitable in Network Marketing. You'll know the basics, you'll cover expenses, and you'll be learning. It will take about three years of consistent part-time effort in order to go full-time. It will take about five years of consistent effort to become a six-figure earner or above. And it will take about seven years of consistent effort to become an expert.

That doesn't mean you can't make more than that in the short-term. Many people do. It just means if you want to KEEP making that kind of money, you need to eventually become an expert.

When you think about it, seven years isn't so bad, especially when a good portion of it is part-time. You're going to be seven years older anyway. You might as well become an expert over that period of time instead of just going through the motions.

How to Learn

Once you make the commitment to focus on your skills, the next thing you need to do is figure out the best ways to learn. One of the best things that ever happened to me was realizing there are no bad experiences and no good experiences, only learning experiences. This was a major breakthrough. In other words, let go of the outcome and focus on what you can learn from every experience. This took so much pressure off me. Instead of always looking for great experiences, I started focusing on how MANY experiences I could have, because the more I had, the more I could learn.

Another attribute of a top earner in MLM is they are what I like to call "an active student." As a professional, they are always learning, always growing, always trying to get better.

Lou Holtz said it best: "In this world you're either growing or you're dying so get in motion and grow."

I think that's true. Never stop learning.

Model Successful Behavior

Try to avoid reinventing the wheel when you get involved in this profession. The hard work has already been done. No matter what company you're in, it's easy to find someone who's very successful. It doesn't matter if it's getting customers, finding prospects, inviting, presenting, following up, closing, getting people started, building for events, or any other skill, there are people in your company right now who have them mastered. And unlike other professions, the successful people in your company are eager to share their secrets! All you need to do is model their behavior and you can begin to enjoy their results.

Study

Audio programs got me started. Back in 1988, someone gave me a bootleg copy of a talk Jim Rohn gave to the Shaklee company. It was called, "The Seed and the Sower," and it rocked my world. I'll bet I listened to that audiocassette in my car 500 times. From there I did some homework on Jim Rohn and purchased his "Challenge to Succeed" audio program. Mr. Rohn gave me hope, but more than that, he gave me direction in my continual personal development. That audio program launched my personal development journey.

Through the years, I continued with dozens of different audio programs, all incredibly helpful in keeping my mind right. There's something magical about audio. It whispers in your ear, reminding you of your dreams, of your potential and how to get there. In addition, it's repetitive. You probably won't read a book over and over, but you'll listen to an audio program over and over, especially if it's entertaining. And it seems like each time it's different—and it is, because YOU are different.

Jim Rohn also taught me to be a reader. No matter what you're trying to learn, there is someone who has devoted their entire life to the subject and is offering it to you for pennies. Take them up on that offer.

In our electronics-focused, attention deficit society, fewer people seem to read books. That's not true for leaders. Ask the top-earning distributors if they are readers. More important-ly, ask them what they are reading. I wasn't much of a reader before I became a Network Marketing professional. But since 1988, I've read an average of about four books a month. Those books have shaped my life and my career for the better. Com-mit to just 10 pages a day and you can read a 300-page book in a month. That's a great start.

Video

Video is another source of great learning. Sometimes I like to watch a training program instead of just listening. It's part of the reason I decided to use video as my main focus at Net-workMarketingPro.com. I found if I create a short video with interesting information every day, people receive tremendous value. If you'd like to check out the hundreds of videos, you can go to http://networkmarketingpro.com. It's free.

Online

The Internet has changed the way we learn and gather information. You can take advantage of online tutorials, watch online videos, attend online webinars, or even watch events "live" with streaming technology.

Events

The best way I know to really internalize life-changing information is to attend live events. As I've already told you, most of my defining moments have come from events. On one side, there is always good information for a person who's listening. On the other side, when you eliminate all of the other distractions in life and just focus, like you do at an event, you have a chance to really hear. Both sides are good.

Be Careful of Distractions

With all of the choices available to you in terms of studying your craft, now, more than ever, you must be careful about what you allow into your mind. People everywhere will try to distract you with their latest and greatest breakthrough and it can be very tempting to jump at all those opportunities. You should be focused on a very narrow range of skills: Finding prospects, inviting, presenting, following up, closing, getting people started right, and promoting events. Make sure you master THOSE skills first before adding anything else to your "to do" list.

Take Action

Almost all of the learning in MLM is in the doing. If you want to learn how to talk to people on the phone, then talk to more people on the phone. If you want to learn how to do a home presentation, then do more home presentations. You will certainly figure it out. That doesn't mean you shouldn't continue to seek knowledge on the skillsets for success in MLM, but it does mean you shouldn't wait for complete knowledge before taking action.

Part of the reason people avoid taking action is they are afraid they'll be embarrassed. If you want to be successful in Network Marketing, you must learn to set that fear aside. Here's why: It's very difficult to look good and get better at the same time. Instead of being afraid of how you look as you're learning and growing, be afraid of not taking action and living a life at a fraction of your potential.

Let me give you a concept that has served me for over 20 years in the area of developing my skills. Back in the early 1990s, a friend and I were searching for a great Network Marketing product. We traveled the country and met with many interesting people. Our journey led us to an organization in Michigan called the High Scope Educational Research Foundation. They had a progressive and proven way to teach children how to learn more effectively.

High Scope has many components, but the one that struck me then is the one I've used to this day, called "plan-do-review." Here's how the company explains the process: "In the plan-do review process, children make plans, carry them out, and reflect on what they have done. In doing so, children learn to take initiative, solve problems, work with others, and accomplish their goals — their play becomes more purposeful and focused. By making plan-do-review a successful and integral part of your classroom's daily routine, you'll learn how you can promote learning and build on children's interests and intrinsic motivation."

While I heard what they were saying on how to use it as a teaching tool for children, the only thing that was rolling around in my mind was how I could use it for myself and for the people in my organization. While things didn't work out for turning the High Scope product into a Network Marketing product, I'll be forever grateful to their organization for helping me and hundreds of thousands of people all over the world to use this concept to build a better business.

Here's how I've used and taught the concept for over 20 years now:

Choose a skill you want to develop.

1. Make a PLAN.

2. DO your plan.

3. REVIEW your results to see how you can do better next time.

Most people don't make a plan, they just charge out and DO. Even more people never REVIEW their results to see how they could improve. Do you see how this connects with no good experiences and no bad experiences, only learning experiences?

1. Make a PLAN.

2. DO your plan.

3. REVIEW your results, good or bad, to see how you can do better next time.

4. Make a better PLAN.

5. DO that better plan.

6. REVIEW those results, good or bad, to see how you can do better next time.

7. Never stop applying plan-do-review and you'll eventually become an expert through trial and error.

This little "secret" to learning in MLM is one of the most powerful I've shared. It's become part of my DNA. I hope the same happens for you.

Teaching

Would it surprise you to know that teaching is one of the best ways to learn? It's true. If you want to really master something, teach it to others. Teaching burns a groove in your brain like nothing else can.

Who do you think gets the most benefit from the daily video shows at NetworkMarketingPro.com? I do! I have to think about it, prepare, and present the message every day, so it helps keep me sharp and on top of my game. The lesson for each of you should be to find someone to teach, even if you just have one person in your group. Start there, and as your group grows, look for more and more opportunities to teach. You'll get the most benefit.

Your Associations

This is another important lesson from Jim Rohn. He taught me the Law of Association that says you'll become the average of the five people you spend the most time with. You'll think how they think, act how they act, talk how they talk, and earn how they earn. Let me tell you something. This law is real. You can't fight it.

I've done three things over the course of my career when it comes to my associations.

First, I've disassociated with the people who were toxic to my life. This isn't an easy decision, but it's an important one. Some people will keep you down permanently.

Second, I've limited my associations with negative people or people who weren't helping me grow in the direction of my dreams. I've just learned to spend less time with those people and more time on positive influences.

And third, I've worked to expand my associations with people who can help me become a better person and a better professional. If you're trying to learn to become an expert in the Network Marketing Profession, doesn't it make sense to find a way to spend more time with the people who have the skills you're looking for?

If this is a little too stressful to think about when you're looking at the five people you're spending your time with right now, here's a little tip: About every six months, one of the people in your five will change. They'll move, get a new job, start a relationship, end a relationship—something will happen. The secret is, when that happens, choose very wisely when you're thinking about who's going to take their place. Most people don't think about this at all. They just let the next person fall into that place. That's a big mistake. Find someone who will push you. Find someone who will inspire you.

I hope these suggestions on the learning process of becoming a professional have been helpful to you. It's okay to dream big, but you also have to be patient. Anything of value takes time. Continue to develop your skills. Become a permanent student. Those skills will make a place for you for the rest of your life.

There's one more concept you need to understand. I've analyzed the top earners in Network Marketing. I've interviewed them and we've become friends. Do you know what they all have in common? They work HARD. Don't get me wrong, they have a great lifestyle and they love what they do, but they work their butts off. If you want big success in MLM, you're going to have to do the same.

Network Marketing isn't about luck, timing, positioning, or signing that magic person who will make you rich. Freedom is possible, but it isn't free. It will take hard work to stay consistent when the world tries to distract you. It will take hard work to learn the skills required for long-term success. It will take hard work to become the leader you were meant to be.

Some people in Network Marketing become unhappy when they realize work is involved. Most of them join for some sort of free ride. When they experience growing pains, they run for the hills. Be different. It might be hard work but it's good work and it's the best way I know for the average person to enjoy true freedom.

CHAPTER TWELVE

It's All Worth It

etwork Marketing can be challenging. It is an emotional experience. The ups and downs can be dramatic. But in the end, for so many reasons, it's all worth it.

The Career You Will Create

If you decide to become a Network Marketing Professional, you will not only create an income for yourself, you'll create a career. I think about this a lot. Consider the skills required to be a doctor, a lawyer, a big company CEO, or even a world-class musician. You're talking about a high level of skill, and a fairly high level of income.

Now consider the skills necessary to become a Network Marketing Professional. They are TINY in comparison! And yet many Network Marketing Professionals enjoy a higher level of income and most certainly a higher degree of freedom.

If you look at any career, there is a barrier of entry (how hard it is to get in) and a long-term benefit (what you get if you do get in). For example, a doctor might have 12 years of school plus an internship. That takes intelligence some of us don't have, money some of us don't have, or even possibly contacts some of us don't have. At the end, they get to enjoy a long-term benefit (although many of them would say the benefit wasn't worth the investment).

There's always a ratio between the barrier of entry and the long-term benefit. There is no question in my mind that of all professions in the world, the profession of Network Marketing has the best ratio when you compare the low barrier of entry with the high long-term return.

One of the best decisions in my life was making a career out of Network Marketing instead of just messing around. Becoming a professional made all the difference, and now it's great fun to spend a good portion of my time helping other people do the same thing.

The Freedom You Will Enjoy

Freedom is an interesting word. When it comes to work, I think we understand the concept, but not the entire meaning. For me, freedom means having choices. It means living the life I want to live instead of the life other people want me to live.

Do you remember the imagination you had as a child? Imagine your life without limits.

- You wake up when you're done sleeping.

- You're doing work that is fulfilling and makes you happy.

- You get to work with people you enjoy.

- You don't have to compromise all the time.

- You work when you feel like working but you also play when you feel like playing.

- You get to spend tons of time with the people who are important to you.

- You are living a big life and not wasting away in a box.

When you get a clear picture of what freedom is all about, you'll find the price you'll need to pay to achieve it in Network Marketing is very low. Facing your fears and living a life that's free is easy. Spending the rest of your days living half a life is hard.

The Lives You Will Touch

It's one thing to create freedom for yourself and your family. It's another thing altogether to help someone else do the same. There are so many people struggling in this world. You have the ability to help people see a bigger picture for themselves. You can give hope to the hopeless. You can encourage their dreams. You can provide them with the inspiration necessary to face and overcome their fears.

One of my greatest joys is to appear in someone else's testimonial. It's great to hear that someone was lost, and in some small way I was able to help them find their way. Network Marketing allows you to do this on a very big scale. Not only can you help one person, but you can help hundreds or even thousands to live a better life. And the exciting thing is, that is just the beginning.

It's just like throwing a rock into a pond. When it hits the water you see the ripples growing larger and larger until they hit every edge of the pond. In Network Marketing, sometimes you don't see all the ripples. You might be aware of the impact you had on one person's life and maybe one or two more ripples, but they keep growing whether you see them or not.

This is why I do what I do. It's why I wrote this book. I know people will be positively impacted and that's a stone thrown into the water. But then they'll make a positive impact on others and the ripples begin, and those people will do the same, and over and over and over again.

With Network Marketing, you really can make a difference.

The People You Will Meet

Network Marketing has introduced me to the most amazing people. This profession gives you a chance not only to expand your group of friends, but also to be able to spend more time with them. You'll never find a more passionate group of entrepreneurs in any other profession. These people love life and spend their time lifting each other up. Here's an example of what that means to me and what it could mean for you. You can name virtually any state in the United States or any other country in the world, and a friend instantly pops into my mind.

Network Marketing has also introduced me to many of my heroes. I've been lucky enough share the stage and become friends with great people, including Anthony Robbins, Brian Tracy, Denis Waitley, the late Stephen Covey, Tom Peters, Les Brown, the late Og Mandino, David Bach, Robert Kiyosaki, Harvey Mackay, Art Williams, Ken Blanchard, Tom Rath, Daniel Pink, Mark Victor Hansen, Jack Canfield, Jeffrey Gitomer, Gary Vaynerchuk, Tom Hopkins, and many, many others. On top of all that, I've been able to learn from more million-dollar MLM earners than I could count. All of them have had a positive impact on my life and my career.

This profession also helped introduce me to my amazing wife Marina. I was in Moscow for a big MLM training event and she was attending that event with her family. Because she could speak multiple languages, she was helping to translate backstage. I was smitten. Our first date was in Red Square at midnight after the event, with the snow softly falling around us. I'll never forget it. We've been together ever since. I'm not saying you'll find the love of your life in MLM, but I AM saying you'll find friendships that will last a lifetime.

The Places You Will See

If you build a large and successful Network Marketing business a few things will happen. First, you'll win some trips that will be trips of a lifetime. Second, you're going to need to support your organization as they expand into every territory or country where your company does business. And third, you're going to have enough money and time to go wherever you'd like.

It's been said that your life can be measured by the number and intensity of your experiences. If that's true, I've already lived a very long life. I've been to every state in the United States with the exception of Alaska, and I'll remedy that soon. I've also been to about 40 countries around the world. I've gone diving at the Great Barrier Reef in Australia, toured the Hagia Sofia in Istanbul, visited the twin towers in Malaysia, boated around James Bond island off the coast of

Thailand, visited the tent cities in Nigeria, ridden the huge Ferris wheel in the port of Singapore, had a private tour of the White House, watched the sun rise on New Year's Day at the Grand Canyon, enjoyed a 30-course meal at the world-famous El Bulli in Spain, cruised through the canals of Amsterdam, ridden a hot air balloon over the Rocky Mountains, rented an entire cruise ship for 2,000 of my friends to sail to the Bahamas, had dinner under the stars on top of the Hotel de Paris in Monaco, visited my heritage in Norway, sailed the Black Sea off the coast of the Ukraine, witnessed the amazing Sistine Chapel in Rome, golfed at St. Andrews in Scotland, watched a World Cup match in Ireland, and prayed at the Wailing Wall in Jerusalem.

ALL of this and so much more was made possible because I embraced the great profession of Network Marketing. The same can happen for you.

The Causes You Can Contribute To

There are lots of worthy causes. You might want to give to your parents or someone else in your family, or to an organization than means something to you. In 2011, I asked Harvey Mackay, a best-selling author as well as a wildly successful businessman and community activist, for his secret to success. He told me this story.

"*Eric, my father sat me down after I graduated from the University of Minnesota at age 21. I was a little bit cocky, going to take on the world, going to start at the top and work my way up. And he said, 'Harvey, 25 percent, one-fourth of your life, starting now, is going to be devoted to volunteerism.' Now I didn't know what that meant, other than I started volunteering for everything. Heart, cancer, United Way, Boy Scouts, March of Dimes, Salvation Army, everything. Let me tell you what that experience has done for me my entire life. By being on all those boards and being involved in all those charities, I became a better communicator. I became a better leader. I became a better salesperson, because all I was doing was raising money for the more than 20 boards that I've been on. I became a better sales manager. And can you imagine how many new people I met by just being a volunteer? My network grew tremendously.*

"*But the biggest thing that happened was my sense of being a citizen of the world. To know that you've helped another human being and to be able to see the results—it's an unbelievable feeling. I'm so thankful to my father because his advice changed my life.* "

This interview changed MY life because it impacted my thinking on contribution. I had always thought there was really only one way to help a worthy cause and that was with your money. But after my conversation with Harvey, I realized there were three ways to help.

The first is with your money. Of course you can write a check, and that's wonderful. Network Marketing can allow you to write bigger checks than you could ever imagine before.

The second is with your time. Like Harvey said, you can dedicate a portion of your life to causes that are important to you. He chose 25 percent. You can choose whatever you'd like, but I'd encourage you to choose. And by time, I don't mean just volunteering few hours here and there at the shelter or something. I mean give your time to creative thinking, raising awareness, and raising money.

And the third is probably most important, and that is with your influence. Take the time you're going to spend on your cause and put all of your influence behind it. Inspire your organization to do something great with you. Encourage your company to get involved. Leverage your network to do great things. You are powerful and more so because of your involvement in Network Marketing. Use that influence for good. It will change your life for the better.

The Person You Will Become in the Process

Network Marketing changed my life for the better because it forced me to become a better person. As a profession, we move products and services to the customers who want them, but our real purpose is much deeper.

At its core, this profession is an incubator for personal growth.

- You'll learn how face your fears.

- You'll learn how to solve problems.

- You'll learn how to feed your mind with positives and protect your mind from negatives.

- You'll learn how to grow stronger.

- You'll learn how to lead.

When I first started out in this profession I did almost everything out of fear. I was afraid I wouldn't succeed. I was afraid I was going to run out of prospects. I was afraid I was going to miss out on the opportunity. But over time, that fear went away. I decided to focus on myself and my skills instead of all the things I couldn't control, and then everything became clear. I learned the true secret of Network Marketing.

The greatest benefit isn't getting what you want. The greatest benefit is what you'll need to become in order to get what you want. I learned what was always there and what has been passed down for ages. The journey is everything.

Thank you for taking this journey with me. Let me conclude by sharing what I say at the end of every Network Marketing Pro video. Ladies and gentlemen, my wish for you is that you decide to become a Network Marketing Professional—you decide to Go Pro—because it is a stone-cold fact that we have *a better way*. Now let's go tell the world.

About the Author

Eric Worre has been a leader in the Network Marketing Profession for over 25 years. In the course of his esteemed career as a top-producing Network Marketing Professional, he has:

- Earned over $15 million

- Built sales organizations totaling over 500,000 distributors in over 60 countries

- Worked as the president of a $200 million direct-selling company

- Co-founded and worked as president of his own company, TPN—The Peoples Network

- Worked as a seven-figure-a-year marketing consultant to the direct-selling industry.

Along the way, Eric has purposefully become an accomplished trainer, and has conducted live events with more than 250,000 people around the world, teaching them how to also become Network Marketing Professionals. He has shared the stage with Anthony Robbins, the late Jim Rohn, Brian Tracy, Denis Waitley, the late Stephen Covey, Tom Peters, Les

Brown, the late Og Mandino, David Bach, Robert Kiyosaki, Harvey Mackay, Art Williams, Ken Blanchard, Tom Rath, Daniel Pink, Mark Victor Hansen, Jack Canfield, Jeffrey Gitomer, Tom Hopkins, and many others.

In 2009, Eric founded NetworkMarketingPro.com, the most-watched training site in the Network Marketing Profession, with an audience in 137 countries around the world. Since its inception, Network Marketing Pro has provided hundreds of free training videos encompassing dozens of interviews with the most iconic and successful Distributors in the world, and the most powerful training events in the Network Marketing Profession.

He ends each of his videos with his trademark statement: "Ladies and gentlemen, my wish for you is that you decide to become a Network Marketing Professional—you decide to Go Pro—because it is a stone-cold fact that we have *a better way*. Now let's go tell the world."